모조지 미색 100g

디자이너의 컬러 팔레트 3

실무에 영감을 더하는 배색 & 톤 컬러 스타일

북토리디자인센터 지음

COLOR SCHEME INSPIRATION

[Introduction]

아름다운 색을 마주할 때, 색은 마음을 움직이기도 하고 기억을 떠올리게도 하며 새로운 아이디어를 만들어 내기도 합니다. 색을 보는 것은 쉽지만, 원하는 색을 고르고 보기 좋은 색의 조합을 만드는 것은 꽤 어렵고 고민이 되는 일입니다.

색 사용에 어려움이 있는 이들이 색을 다루는 데 도움이 되고자 만들어진 이 책은 어떻게 색을 선택하면 좋을지에 대한 물음과 어떤 배색으로 사용할지에 대한 고민에 답합니다. 사랑스러움, 즐거움, 고독과 같은 감정을 표현하기 위한 추상적인 이미지나 마카롱, 런던, 크리스마스와 같이 구체적인 이미지가 연상되는 이미지 등 다양한 테마를 선정하여, 어울리는 배색과 색의 이미지를 소개합니다.

본문에 제시된 이미지와 색상은 연관된 테마로 색을 사용하고자 할 때 아이디어나 영감을 주는 역할을 할 것입니다. 7개 섹션에 60개 테마로 구성되어 총 300가지의 컬러 팔레트와 내용 및 레이아웃 디자인 샘플이 수록되어 있습니다. 또한, 종이의 종류에 따라 색 발현 및 인쇄성이 다르므로 가장 많이 사용하는 3종의 본문 종이를 선택하여 CMS(Color Management System) 관리하에 인쇄한 후, 용지별 인쇄 차이를 확인할 수 있도록 총 3권의 책으로 구성하였습니다.

기업의 디자인 및 개인의 라이프 스타일까지 다양한 방면에서 색의 사용은 점점 더 주목받고 있습니다. 디자인 및 창작 활동을 하는 전문가뿐 아니라 감각적인 센스를 발휘하고 싶은 모두의 일상에, 특별한 스토리를 만드는 컬러의 일부로 이 책이 활용되기를 바랍니다.

[인쇄 정보]

인　　　쇄　BOOKTORY
인 쇄 장 비　RMGT 1050TP 8color
컬 러 인 증　G7 Master
ICC Profile　GRACoL2013_CRPC6

[용지 정보]

제 지 사　한솔제지
제 품 명　미색백상지
평　　　량　본문100g/m²
색　　　상　연미(S)색

자연스러운 미색 백상지입니다. 전반적으로 노란색이 섞인 톤으로 보이며 눈의 피로도를 덜어줍니다.

[잉크 정보]

제 조 사　(주)디어스아이
제 품 명　PLUS KLEENTEC 적, 청, 황, 흑

디자이너의 컬러 팔레트 3

실무에 영감을 더하는 배색 & 톤 컬러 스타일

[색상 모드와 색상 값에 대한 안내]

이 책에 표기한 색상 코드 수치 값은 해당 콘텐츠의 각 이미지에 속한 색의 일부를 기준으로 작성되었습니다. 게재된 CMYK와 RGB 수치는 농도 값일 뿐 색상 값은 아니므로, 사용된 프로그램(Adobe InDsign)의 색상 설정이 다르면 같은 수치라 하더라도 완전히 동일한 색상은 아닐 수 있습니다. 또한, 사용자의 모니터 환경 및 캘리브레이션 여부와 재현 환경(인쇄되는 소재나 표시 환경)에 따라서도 색상은 미묘하게 다를 수 있으니 참고 자료로 사용하길 권장합니다.

컬러팔레트 및 색상설정 프리셋(BOOKTORY_Coated)
오른쪽 QR코드를 통해 다운로드 받을 수 있습니다.

[색이름 및 콘텐츠 내용에 대한 안내]

이 책에 게재한 모든 내용은 보호를 받는 저작물이므로 무단 전재와 무단 복제를 금합니다.

- 색이름은 컬러 리서치 값을 따르며, 이름이 같아도 색조(Tone)는 조금씩 다를 수 있습니다.
- 콘텐츠를 설명하는 내용(한글, 영문)은 모두 창작물이며, 일부 사전적 의미가 포함되어 있습니다.
- 책에 사용된 이미지는 Getty Images Bank의 유료 콘텐츠입니다.

[이 책의 내용 및 디자인은 아래의 Adobe 인디자인프로그램의 색상 설정 환경에서 작업되었습니다.]

Adobe InDesign → 상단 메뉴 → 편집 → 색상 설정

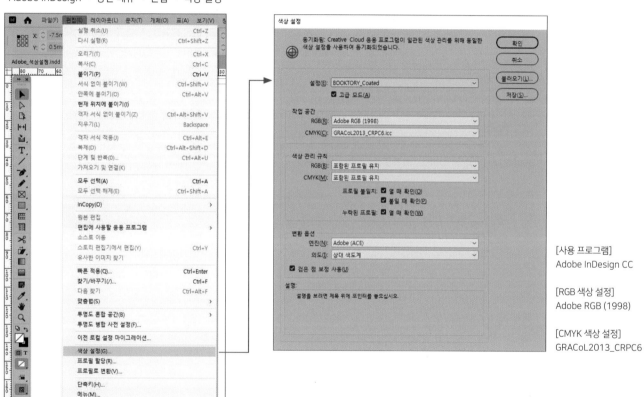

[사용 프로그램]
Adobe InDesign CC

[RGB 색상 설정]
Adobe RGB (1998)

[CMYK 색상 설정]
GRACoL2013_CRPC6

COLOR SYSTEM
색 체계

색상 (Hue)

색상은 색의 가장 명백한 특징이다. 색상은 고명도, 고채도인 순색의 특정한 색을 묘사한다. 일반적으로 색상은 유채색에 있는 빨강, 주황, 노랑, 초록, 파랑, 보라와 같은 색의 이름으로 구별된다.

| Red | Orange | Yellow | Green | Blue | Purple |

명도 (Value)

명도는 색을 구별하는 감각적인 요소 중 하나로 빛의 파장에 의해 느끼는 색의 밝고 어두운 정도를 나타낸다. 밝은 정도에 따라 고명도, 중명도, 저명도로 구분하며 색의 가볍고 무거운 정도, 부드럽고 강한 정도를 표현한다.

고명도 ←—————————————————————→ 저명도

채도 (Saturation)

채도는 색의 선명도와 강도를 나타낸다. 색의 맑고 탁함, 강하고 약함을 표현하며 순색의 정도에 따라 고채도, 중채도, 저채도로 구분한다. 순색일수록 채도가 높고 색이 선명하며, 무채색이나 다른 색이 섞일수록 탁하고 어두워진다.

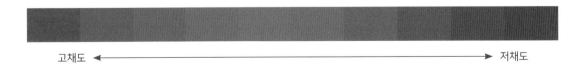

고채도 ←—————————————————————→ 저채도

색상 모델 (Color Models)

RGB와 CMYK는 가산 혼합과 감산 혼합 개념을 기반으로 하는 두 가지 색상 모델이며, 다양한 색상을 재현하는 주요 방법이다. 가산 혼합은 빛을 방출하거나 방사하는 모든 색과 함께 작용한다. 서로 다른 파장의 빛의 혼합은 다른 색을 만들고, 빛이 첨가될수록 색은 더 밝고 가벼워진다. 감산 혼합은 반사된 빛에 기초해서 작용한다. 빛을 밀어내기보다는 특정한 색소가 다른 파장의 빛을 반사하는 방법이 눈으로 보이는 색을 결정한다.

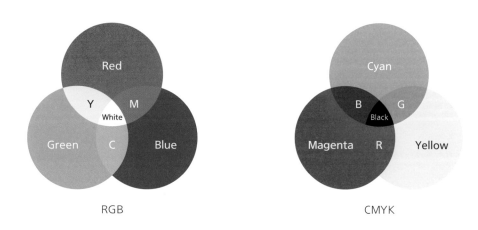

RGB

CMYK

RGB

RGB는 빛의 3원색인 빨강, 초록, 파랑을 의미한다. RGB 색상 모델은 컴퓨터 모니터, TV 또는 다른 화면 장치에 이미지를 표시하는 데 사용되는 가산 혼합 모델이다. 각 색상은 0~255 범위의 값으로 표시된다.

CMYK

CMYK는 청록, 자홍, 노랑의 3원색에 검정을 추가한 것이다. RGB와는 다르게 CMY로 완벽한 검정색을 만들 수 없어 K(블랙)이 필요하다. CMYK 색상 모델은 인쇄물, 그림, 사진 및 기타 물리적 매체에 잉크를 사용하여 표현되는 감산 혼합 모델이다. 각 색상은 0~100% 사이의 백분율 값으로 표시된다.

COLOR WHEEL
색상환

1차색 (PRIMARY COLORS)
1차색은 RGB 컬러 모델의 빨강, 초록, 파랑과 CMY 컬러 모델의 청록, 자홍, 노랑으로 구성한다. 이 기본색상은 다른 색상을 혼합해서 만들어낼 수 없다. 각 컬러 모델의 기본 3가지 색은 광범위한 색상 범위나 색 공간의 구성 요소로, 이 색을 혼합해 2차 색상과 3차 색상, 나아가 그 사이의 중간 색상을 만든다.

2차색 (SECONDARY COLORS)
2차색은 서로 다른 2가지 1차색을 같은 비율로 혼합해서 만든다. 노랑과 파랑을 혼합하면 초록, 노랑과 빨강을 혼합하면 주황, 파랑과 빨강을 혼합하면 보라가 만들어진다. 색상환에서 2차색은 그 색상을 만드는 데 사용된 2가지 1차색의 중간에 위치하고 등거리에 있다. 2차 색상 3가지가 모여 역정삼각형을 만든다.

3차색 (TERTIARY COLORS)
3차색은 1차색과 인접한 2차색을 혼합하여 만들어진다. 예를 들어, CMY 컬러 모델의 1차색인 노랑과 2차색인 초록을 혼합하면 황록이 만들어지게 된다. 각 3차색의 이름은 인접한 2차색과 결합한 1차색의 이름으로 시작한다.

───── **12-COLOR WHEEL** ─────

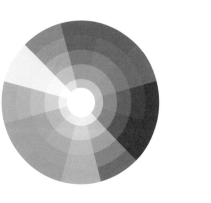

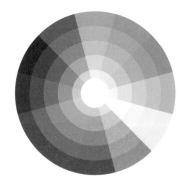

RGB

CMY

PRIMARY COLORS

Red (●)
Green (●)
Blue (●)

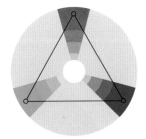

Cyan (●)
Magenta (●)
Yellow ( )

SECONDARY COLORS

Red + Green = Yellow ( )
Green + Blue = Cyan (●)
Blue + Red = Magenta (●)

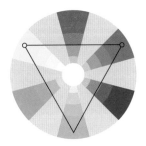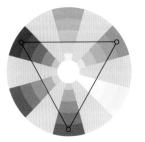

Magenta + Cyan = Blue (●)
Yellow + Magenta = Red (●)
Cyan + Yellow = Green (●)

TERTIARY COLORS

Red + Yellow = Orange (●)
Yellow + Green = Chartreuse (●)
Green + Cyan = Spring Green (●)
Cyan + Blue = Azure (●)
Blue + Magenta = Violet (●)
Magenta + Red = Rose (●)

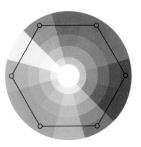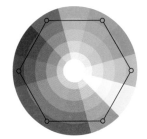

Cyan + Blue = Azure (●)
Blue + Magenta = Violet (●)
Magenta + Red = Rose (●)
Red + Yellow = Orange (●)
Yellow + Green = Chartreuse (●)
Green + Cyan = Spring Green (●)

COLOR SCHEMES
배색 방법

01 MONOCHROMATIC
동일색

한 가지 색상을 기초로 한 배색, 단일 색상 배색이라고도 한다.
명도나 채도의 차이를 이용해 변화를 주면 효과적이다.

02 ANALOGOUS
인접색

색상환에서 30도 범위 내로 인접한 색상 간의 배색 조화,
인접색 배색이라고도 한다. 명도나 채도에 크게 변화를 주어
대립된 요소로 배색하는 것이 바람직하다.

03 TRIADIC
정삼각색

색상환을 6등분 하여 색 차이가 60도인 유사색을 배색한다.
전체적으로 색상 차이가 크지 않으면서 각각의 색감을 느낄 수
있어 매력적인 조화를 이룬다.

04 SQUARE
정사각색

색상환을 4등분 하여 색 차이가 90도인 배색 관계로
화려한 분위기를 연출한다.

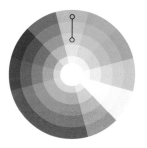

MONOCHROMATIC
동일색

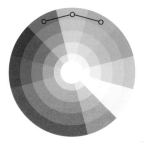

ANALOGOUS
인접색

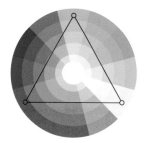

TRIADIC
정삼각색

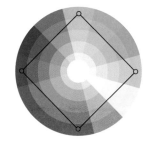

SQUARE
정사각색

COMPLEMENTARY
보색

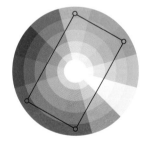

SPLIT COMPLEMENTARY
인접보색

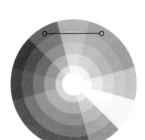

DIAD
디아드

TETRAD (RECTANGLE)
사각색

COMPLEMENTARY 05
보색

색상환에서 정반대에 위치한 두 가지 색의 배색으로
반대색 배색이라고도 한다.

SPLIT COMPLEMENTARY 06
인접보색

한 개의 색상과 그 보색의 양옆에 있는 색상들 간의
배색 조화로 준보색 배색이라고도 한다.

DIAD 07
디아드

디아드 컬러 배합은 색상환에서 하나의 컬러를 사이에 둔
양옆의 색상을 사용하는 것을 말한다.

TETRAD (RECTANGLE) 08
사각색

색상환과 직사각형의 중심축을 포개었을 때
직사각형의 각 모서리에 닿은 4가지 색을 말한다.

| Contents

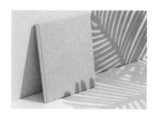
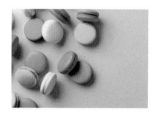

NATURAL

NATURAL

Greenery

Pure

Fresh

Lush

Organic

Wild

Greenery

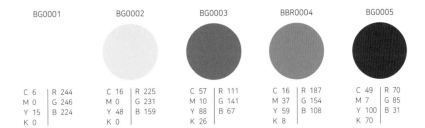

BG0001	BG0002	BG0003	BBR0004	BG0005
C 6 | R 244	C 16 | R 225	C 57 | R 111	C 16 | R 187	C 49 | R 70
M 0 | G 246	M 0 | G 231	M 10 | G 141	M 37 | G 154	M 7 | G 85
Y 15 | B 224	Y 48 | B 159	Y 88 | B 67	Y 59 | B 108	Y 100 | B 31
K 0	K 0	K 26	K 8	K 70

Color Palette - Light Mint Green, Light Yellow Green, Green, Light Brown, Dark Green
밝은 초록색 계열의 배색은 싱그럽고 생동감 넘치는 인상을 줍니다.
그린과 브라운 색상을 조합하면 편안하고 내추럴한 이미지를 연출할 수 있습니다.

2 color combination   3 color combination   4 color combination

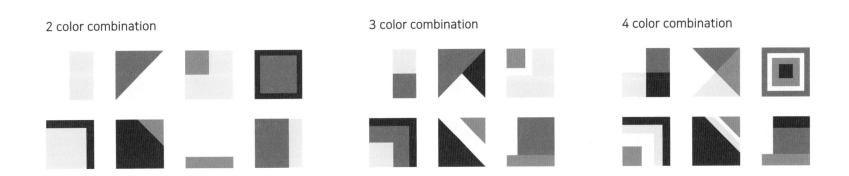

Eating Healthy everyday

What do you see when you choose food? Are you buying it based on the design, taste, quantity, and price of the container? The more careful you look at each one, the more you can protect your health and the environment.

Green Food

As a green food that helps regenerate cells, the green color of fruits and vegetables acts on the sympathetic nerves, activating the function of kidney liver and detoxifying pollutants.

Herb is a flavored or fragrant plant used as a condiment to flavor food or as a garnish for cooking. It is also used as a medicine or perfume and is drunk as tea. Herbs are mainly leaves or flowers, while spices are mainly used by drying berries, seeds, roots and stems. Recently, various foods that use mugwort as a herb have been developed.

Rosemary

How to Design Lifestyle & Eating Habits

Good, Tasty

Fresh vegetables, fruits, and milk not only contain many healthy ingredients, but also help release sodium from the body.

Pure

BB0006	BY0007	BG0008	BB0009	BB0010

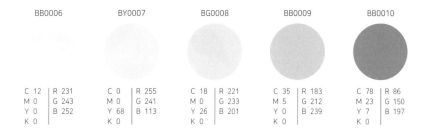

C 12	R 231	C 0	R 255	C 18	R 221	C 35	R 183	C 78	R 86
M 0	G 243	M 0	G 241	M 0	G 233	M 5	G 212	M 23	G 150
Y 0	B 252	Y 68	B 113	Y 26	B 201	Y 0	B 239	Y 7	B 197
K 0		K 0		K 0		K 0		K 0	

Color Palette - Light Blue, Light Yellow, Light Mint Green, Sky Blue, Cerulean Blue
명도와 채도가 높은 밝은 톤 색상은 산뜻하고 청량한 느낌을 줍니다.
명도가 낮은 짙은 색을 조합하여 대비를 높히면 투명하고 깨끗한 이미지가 강조됩니다.

2 color combination

3 color combination

4 color combination

GOOD DESIGN
PROJECTS

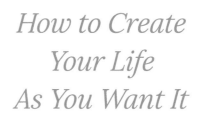

How to Create
Your Life
As You Want It

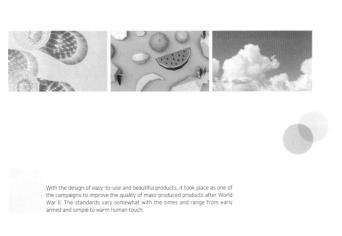

With the design of easy-to-use and beautiful products, it took place as one of the campaigns to improve the quality of mass-produced products after World War II. The standards vary somewhat with the times and range from early armed and simple to warm human touch.

Architecture &
Housing Design

Architects synthesize the requirements of various subjects and plans through creative enthusiasm and extensive control, coordination, and arrangement skills.

Fresh

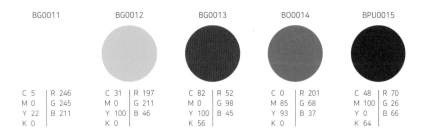

	BG0012		BG0013		BO0014		BPU0015	

C 5	R 246	C 31	R 197	C 82	R 52	C 0	R 201	C 48	R 70
M 0	G 245	M 0	G 211	M 0	G 98	M 85	G 68	M 100	G 26
Y 22	B 211	Y 100	B 46	Y 100	B 45	Y 93	B 37	Y 0	B 66
K 0		K 0		K 56		K 0		K 64	

Color Palette - Light Lime Green, Yellow Green, Deep Green, Orange, Deep Purple
녹황색 채소의 초록색과 붉은색은 신선한 이미지를 떠오르게 합니다.
그린 계열 색상에 레드와 퍼플로 보색 대비를 주면 산뜻함이 강조됩니다.

2 color combination

3 color combination

4 color combination

What do you see when you choose food? Are you buying it based on the design, taste, quantity, and price of the container? The more careful you look at each one, the more you can protect your health and the environment.

Eating Healthy everyday

You can maintain a healthy eating habits by making seasonal foods, and It is important to learn the balanced eating habits of each nutrient.

CHOOSING THE RIGHT FRESH FOOD FOR OUR BODY

Fresh vegetables, fruits, and milk not only contain many healthy ingredients, but also help release sodium from the body.

PARSLEY, LAVENDER, BASIL, THYME, ROSEMARY

Herbs are different from vegetables in that they use small amounts to provide flavor or flavor.

Herb

Herb is a flavored or fragrant plant used as a condiment to flavor food or as a garnish for cooking. It is also used as a medicine or perfume and is drunk as tea. Herbs are mainly leaves or flowers, while spices are mainly used by drying berries, seeds, roots and stems. Recently, various foods that use mugwort as a herb have been developed.

How to eat healthy food

As a green food that helps regenerate cells, the green color of fruits and vegetables acts on the sympathetic nerves, activating the function of kidney liver and detoxifying pollutants.

Lush

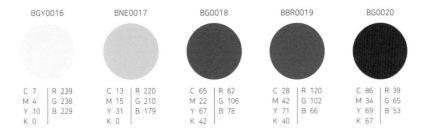

BGY0016	BNE0017	BG0018	BBR0019	BG0020
C 7 R 239	C 13 R 220	C 65 R 82	C 28 R 120	C 86 R 39
M 4 G 238	M 15 G 210	M 22 G 106	M 42 G 102	M 34 G 65
Y 10 B 229	Y 31 B 179	Y 67 B 78	Y 71 B 66	Y 69 B 53
K 0	K 0	K 42	K 40	K 67

Color Palette - Light Green Gray, Beige, Dark Green, Donkey Brown, Black Green
푸른 잎이 무성한 숲속은 짙은 초록의 나무들로 가득합니다.
명도와 채도가 낮은 그린, 브라운 계열의 배색은 숲속처럼 고요하고 안정적인 이미지를 표현합니다.

2 color combination

3 color combination

4 color combination

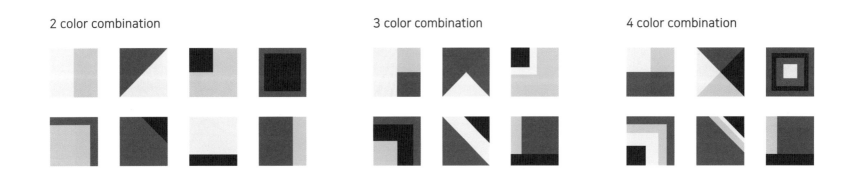

01

forest

A forest is a village where plants live together. People make a lot of efforts to make the forest green, such as planting trees and not throwing away trash. The forest keeps the air clean. Leaves suck up pollutants such as fine dust and sulfur dioxide that float in the air. These pollutants melt into rainwater and fall to the ground when it rains and are purified as they flow through the forest.

02

forest is an area of large and small trees

03

Forests control the amount of water to reduce the damage from floods and droughts. The roots of grass or trees are densely spread out in the soil. There are many small spaces between these roots and the soil.

HOW TO PRESERVE OUR FORESTS

Human beings have made civilization by relying heavily on forests. Humans have also made efforts to preserve forests, but have also destroyed forests for many reasons. Forest changes have had a great impact on people's lives. Before agriculture began, mankind had been living in the forest by hunting and gathering. But as we began farming, mankind slowly began to destroy forests by turning them into farmland. Although forests have turned into farmland, the role of forests in agricultural society has become more important.

Organic

BW0021	BNE0022	BG0023	BBR0024	BPU0025

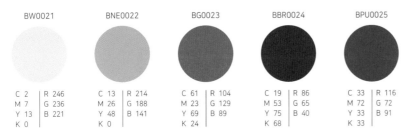

C 2	R 246	C 13	R 214	C 61	R 104	C 19	R 86	C 33	R 116				
M 7	G 236	M 26	G 188	M 23	G 129	M 53	G 65	M 72	G 72				
Y 13	B 221	Y 48	B 141	Y 69	B 89	Y 75	B 40	Y 33	B 91				
K 0		K 0		K 24		K 68		K 33					

Color Palette - Ivory, Tan Beige, Dark Yellow Green, Deep Brown, Dark Purple
녹색과 갈색의 조합은 가공하지 않은 자연의 재료를 떠올리게 합니다.
그린과 브라운 배색에 보색으로 포인트 컬러를 주면 컬러에 생동감이 더해집니다.

2 color combination

3 color combination

4 color combination

Why do consumers buy organic food

What do you see when you choose food? Are you buying it based on the design, taste, quantity, and price of the container? The more careful you look at each one, the more you can protect your health and the environment. Why do consumers buy organic food at a relatively higher price? In addition to the argument that organic food contributes more to health than ordinary food, the trend of organic food can be seen as a cultural, social and psychological outcome.

YOUR PERSONAL EATING HABITS

You can maintain a healthy eating habits by making seasonal foods, and It is important to learn the balanced eating habits of each nutrient.

CHOOSING THE FRESH FOOD FOR OUR BODY

Fresh vegetables, fruits, and milk not only contain many healthy ingredients, but also help release sodium from the body.

Wild

BGY0026	BGY0027	BNE0028	BBR0029	BBR0030
C 10 R 230	C 22 R 202	C 5 R 234	C 35 R 119	C 29 R 88
M 8 G 229	M 15 G 204	M 17 G 212	M 45 G 104	M 61 G 64
Y 7 B 229	Y 14 B 207	Y 33 B 174	Y 61 B 81	Y 74 B 45
K 0	K 0	K 0	K 34	K 60

Color Palette - Light Pale Gray, Light Blue Gray, Cream Beige, Walnut Brown, Deep Brown
그레이와 저채도의 브라운 색상 조합은 고요하고 차가운 느낌을 줍니다.
명도가 높은 웜 톤 계열 색상을 포인트로 사용하면 따뜻한 느낌이 더해지는 효과를 볼 수 있습니다.

2 color combination

3 color combination

4 color combination

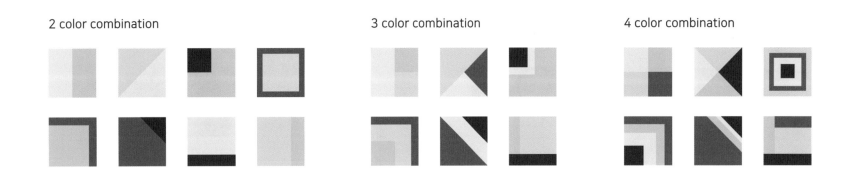

HOW TO SURVIVE IN THE DESERT

Oasis is where people survive in the desert. The water in the oasis is not made by rainwater. Rain or snow melted from afar into groundwater.

01

Wild animals are birds, deer, squirrels, fish, and snakes, etc. that grow on their own in the mountains and fields. In order to manage and protect these wild animals well, food, water, shelter, etc. must be provided. Meanwhile, when the number of wild animals increases too much, they can also be hunted down to reduce the number of wild animals.

FIND OUT HOW ANIMALS AND PLANTS SURVIVE IN THE HOT DESERT

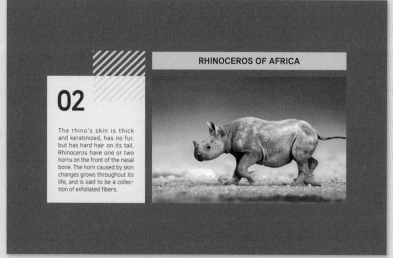

RHINOCEROS OF AFRICA

02

The rhino's skin is thick and keratinized, has no fur, but has hard hair on its tail. Rhinoceros have one or two horns on the front of the nasal bone. The horn caused by skin changes grows throughout its life, and is said to be a collection of exfoliated fibers.

EMOTIONAL

EMOTIONAL

Delicate

Dreamy

Sweet

Soft

Solitude

Tranquility

Joyful

Romantic

Lovely

Calm

Dark

Delicate

BW0031	BNE0032	BG0033	BG0034	BBR0035

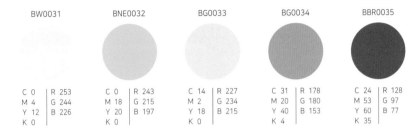

C 0	R 253	C 0	R 243	C 14	R 227	C 31	R 178	C 24	R 128
M 4	G 244	M 18	G 215	M 2	G 234	M 20	G 180	M 53	G 97
Y 12	B 226	Y 20	B 197	Y 18	B 215	Y 40	B 153	Y 60	B 77
K 0		K 0		K 0		K 4		K 35	

Color Palette - Ivory, Soft Peach, Light Mint Green, Cottage Green, Brown

Delicate는 향기·빛 등이 '은은하다' 또는 '아름다운, 섬세한, 연약한, 여린'을 의미합니다.
아이보리와 밝은 핑크, 그린의 소프트한 색상 배색은 부드럽고 섬세한 분위기를 연출할 수 있습니다.

2 color combination

3 color combination

4 color combination

The language of flowers

Since ancient times, flowers have been used as symbols and signs for various ethnic groups, religions, and folklore. Since flowers change their feelings depending on the place, time, and the viewer's feelings, people from various countries around the world create flower words to convey each other's feelings. In France, in addition to the expression 'The language of flowers', it is also called 'a word of something'.

Baby's breath

Many branches divide and small white flowers bloom in groups from summer to autumn. Five petals, with concave ends. The most popular variety is white flowers, which have the flower language of pure heart, promise, and fruit of love. White and small flowers make roses and carnations stand out, and are usually used for ornamental or flower arrangement.

COMMON GYPSOPHILA

TARAXACUM PLATYCARPUM

Dandelion

Grow in a sunny spot in the field. No stem, leaves clump from the roots and spread sideways. In Europe, leaves are eaten as salads, and in New Zealand, roots are used as substitutes for coffee.

Wildflowe, blooming in nature

Wild flowers grow and bloom on their own in the mountains and fields.

Dreamy

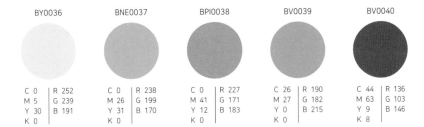

BY0036	BNE0037	BPI0038	BV0039	BV0040
C 0 R 252	C 0 R 238	C 0 R 227	C 26 R 190	C 44 R 136
M 5 G 239	M 26 G 199	M 41 G 171	M 27 G 182	M 63 G 103
Y 30 B 191	Y 31 B 170	Y 12 B 183	Y 0 B 215	Y 9 B 146
K 0	K 0	K 0	K 0	K 8

Color Palette - Cream Yellow, Soft Coral, Pink, Lavendar Violet, Violet

황홀하고 달콤한 꿈속에선 현실과 다른 환상적인 세계가 펼쳐집니다.
웜 톤의 파스텔컬러와 바이올렛 색상 배색은 따뜻하고 포근하면서 몽환적인 느낌을 줍니다.

2 color combination   3 color combination   4 color combination

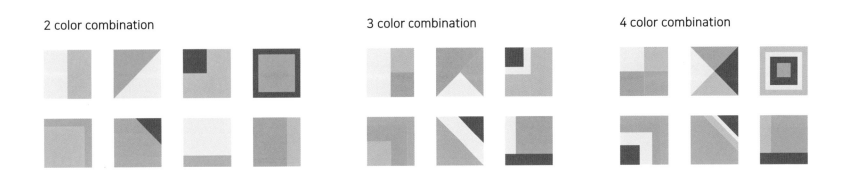

AMUSEMENT
P A R K

An amusement park means a creative leisure space created by discovering materials that can impress and entertain users in various fields, being equipped for functions such as entertainment, recreation, education, and experience, and planning play programs and characters in unison.

M E R R Y -
GO-ROUND

Mary Go Round or Round About is a British name and carousel in the United States. This means a horse race that was popular in the West in the 17th century, and was designed as a practice tool for throwing spears on horses. At that time, the horse was given a fancy harness, which was named after the merry-go-round with similar harnesses. A round platform installed slightly above the ground has a wooden-horse-shaped seat and rotates with the platform by the power of the motor in the center.

YOU CAN FEEL
LOTS OF EXCITEMENT
IN THE
AMUSEMENT
PARK

The wooden horse moves up and down at the same time, and the riding children experience the pleasure of riding a horse.

A ferris wheel is a type of amusement equipment, with several small rooms hanging around a huge wheel and designed to look far away according to the rotation of the wheel.

Sweet

BW0041	BNE0042	BPI0043	BG0044	BPI0045

C 3 — R 245	C 0 — R 245	C 0 — R 233	C 30 — R 193	C 0 — R 210
M 6 — G 238	M 15 — G 221	M 32 — G 189	M 6 — G 211	M 71 — G 104
Y 11 — B 226	Y 21 — B 198	Y 10 — B 197	Y 28 — B 190	Y 37 — B 117
K 0	K 0	K 0	K 0	K 0

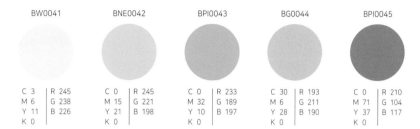

Color Palette - Linen White, Soft Apricot, Soft Pink, Light Pale Green, Pink Grapefruit
파스텔 톤 컬러 배색은 부드럽고 달콤한 이미지를 떠오르게 합니다.
소프트한 핑크 색상을 베이스로 그린 컬러를 조합하면 부드럽고 발랄한 느낌을 줍니다.

2 color combination

3 color combination

4 color combination

Pledge of Love

A wedding ceremony is a ceremony in which a man and a woman make a vow of marriage in the presence of their family members, close relatives and neighbors, Weddings are often held in combination with traditional customs, customs, or religious ceremonies, and can be divided into various ways, such as using wedding halls or following their own religious rituals,

Bride's bouquet

Bouquet means 'bunch or bundle' in French, Before the wedding, the groom made a bouquet of flowers from nature and gave them to the bride, One of them was given to the groom,

Wedding cakes will be handed out to guests by the bride and groom, who will help them, and the bride will cut the knife and hand it out to them, which is the first collaboration between the two, Wedding cakes are decorated with grooms, brides, carriages, hearts, etc. It was not used much in the early days except for castella, but recently a luxurious cake has been made and used for some wedding reception,

Wedding Cakes

flower decorations sweets wedding rings champagne that shine the wedding

House wedding is a party style wedding in a small space decorated like a mansion, inviting only small guests;

Soft

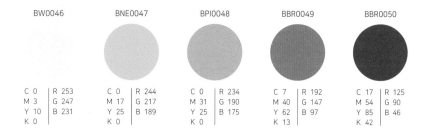

	BW0046		BNE0047		BPI0048		BBR0049		BBR0050
C 0	R 253	C 0	R 244	C 0	R 234	C 7	R 192	C 17	R 125
M 3	G 247	M 17	G 217	M 31	G 190	M 40	G 147	M 54	G 90
Y 10	B 231	Y 25	B 189	Y 25	B 175	Y 62	B 97	Y 85	B 46
K 0		K 0		K 0		K 13		K 42	

Color Palette - Ivory, Soft Apricot, Salmon Pink, Sandy Brown, Sienna Brown
웜 톤의 파스텔컬러는 포근하고 따뜻한 느낌을 줍니다.
아이보리와 핑크, 브라운 배색을 사용하면 부드럽고 편안한 분위기를 연출할 수 있습니다.

2 color combination

3 color combination

4 color combination

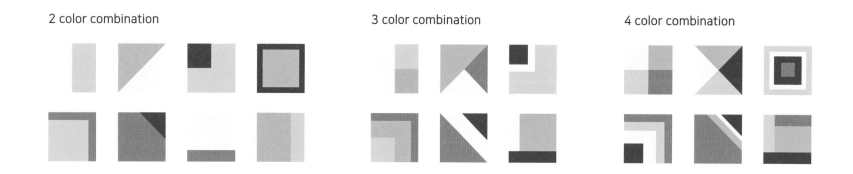

Knit

**Why do consumers
buy knitwear**

Knitware includes both hand-knitted and knitted fabrics. In a narrow sense, it also refers to knitted outerwear, such as sweaters, jackets, coats, etc. Knitware usually has advantages such as not binding the body due to its rich elasticity and soft touch, being good for keeping warm due to its large airworthiness, and not having to iron it because it is not wrinkled well. In Europe and the United States, knitwear has emerged as a fashion that has drawn attention from the fashion world since the early 1900s.

Soft warm fabric, microfiber

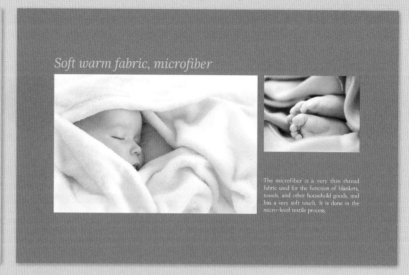

The microfiber is a very thin thread fabric, used for the function of blankets, towels, and other household goods, and has a very soft touch. It is done in the micro-level textile process.

*Knitwear,
knit interior
in our
daily lives*

How to
take good
care of
knitwear

Although knitwear is said to be highly flexible, it should not be handled roughly when worn and undressed. After wearing it, immediately walk on the hanger or back of the chair to release body temperature or moisture, shake it 3-4 times to remove dust and store it loosely. Hanging on a hanger is easy to spoil the shape of the knitwear, so be careful.

Solitude

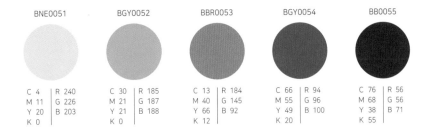

BNE0051	BGY0052	BBR0053	BGY0054	BB0055
C 4 R 240	C 30 R 185	C 13 R 184	C 66 R 94	C 76 R 56
M 11 G 226	M 21 G 187	M 40 G 145	M 55 G 96	M 68 G 56
Y 20 B 203	Y 21 B 188	Y 66 B 92	Y 49 B 100	Y 38 B 71
K 0	K 0	K 12	K 20	K 55

Color Palette - Light Beige, Light Blue Gray, Yellow Brown, Dark Gray, Midnight Blue
Solitude는 온전히 홀로 머무는 시간에서의 '즐거운 고독'을 의미합니다.
차갑고 지적인 그레이와 네이비 배색에, 베이지와 브라운으로 포근함과 안정감을 더해줍니다.

2 color combination

3 color combination

4 color combination

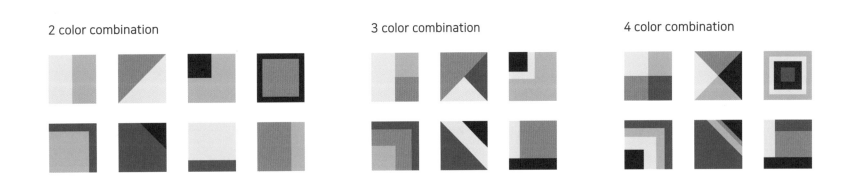

A Good Place to Travel Alone

A GOOD WAY TO TRAVEL ALONE

You can learn how to love nature through hiking, and you can cultivate a healthy body and spirit of self-determination through climbing. Mountain climbing has the effect of strengthening the lower body, improving cardiopulmonary functions, promoting metabolism, and relieving various stresses.

The meaning of camping is 'cooperative life among comrades', and it is meaningful to build friendly human relationships through simple cooperative life in nature, and to train the body as well as to learn from nature through hiking, swimming, fishing and other outdoor activities.

TO VISIT A MUSEUM OR ART GALLERY ALONE

WHAT AND HOW WILL YOU ENJOY IT

The museum defines it as "a permanent public facility built for the purpose of public display for the purpose of public education and entertainment by preserving and studying collections of art, history, science and technology, and materials and specimens of cultural value, such as botanical gardens, zoos, and aquariums, in various ways."

TRAVELING ALONE

Even if you travel, it will be important how you do it. Travelers are active. Travelers search for people, for adventure, and for experience. On the other hand, tourists are passive. Tourists expect interesting things to happen. Traveling alone should be a traveler, not a tourist.

Tranquility

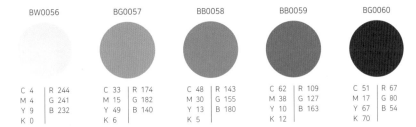

BW0056	BG0057	BB0058	BB0059	BG0060
C 4 / R 244	C 33 / R 174	C 48 / R 143	C 62 / R 109	C 51 / R 67
M 4 / G 241	M 15 / G 182	M 30 / G 155	M 38 / G 127	M 17 / G 80
Y 9 / B 232	Y 49 / B 140	Y 13 / B 180	Y 10 / B 163	Y 67 / B 54
K 0	K 6	K 5	K 12	K 70

Color Palette - Linen White, Pale Green, Gray Blue, Steel Blue, Dark Green
Tranquility는 고요한 바다와 같이 정적이 흐르는 시간의 '평온과 안락'을 의미합니다.
채도가 낮은 그린과 블루 톤 색상 배색은 차분하고 안정된 이미지를 표현하는 데 어울립니다.

2 color combination   3 color combination   4 color combination

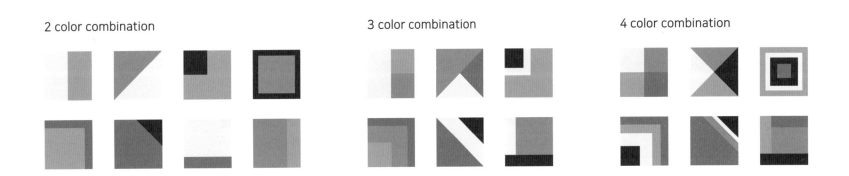

Trust yourself. Then nothing will stop you.

What we think determines who we are.
If we can dream, we can achieve it. Have a dream and hope.

THE ONLY WAY TO FIND TRUE HAPPINESS

What is important to find happiness is to find the right place to be comfortable in the way I am. If there is no such place, it is a good idea to create a place where you can be recognized for your value even if you exist as yourself.

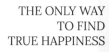

It is entirely up to us to make the opportunity the center of my life and to grow the branches of my dreams. Opportunities come to those who eagerly prepare and dream grandly. If you sincerely strive to make your dream a reality, you will surely have the opportunity to fulfill your dream. Don't be afraid of failure and try to do it.

CALM *and* SLOWLY

Everyone has their own place in the world, whether they choose or not, and plays an important role in their own way. Time flies fast over us, but if you live slowly with peace of mind, one day happiness will quietly sink beside you.

Gift for my tranquil soul

It's a life in the dust, but my own way of healing the soul by living preciously and beautifully.

41

Joyful

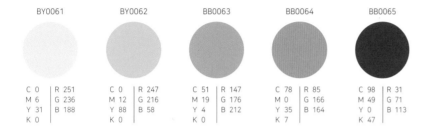

BY0061	BY0062	BB0063	BB0064	BB0065
C 0 R 251	C 0 R 247	C 51 R 147	C 78 R 85	C 98 R 31
M 6 G 236	M 12 G 216	M 19 G 176	M 0 G 166	M 49 G 71
Y 31 B 188	Y 88 B 58	Y 4 B 212	Y 35 B 164	Y 0 B 113
K 0	K 0	K 0	K 7	K 47

Color Palette - Cream Yellow, Canary Yellow, Light Cerulean Blue, Turquoise Blue, Indigo Blue
옐로와 블루 색상 조합은 보색 대비 배색으로 선명한 느낌을 줍니다.
채도가 높은 옐로, 블루, 그린 배색은 밝고 명랑한 분위기를 연출합니다.

2 color combination

3 color combination

4 color combination

by the sea

together

swimsuit, easy-to-work-clothes, life jackets, colored glasses, hats, sand play, ball play, wind surfing, water play, swimming, sand beach, waves, rocky island, parasols, mats, etc.

On a hot summer day, we wear swimsuits and jump into the cool sea. Under the cold, transparent sea, we can see fish and seaweed, and we ride the waves and have fun in the water. When we get tired of playing in the water, we eat barbecue and sweet things, and go back into the sea before sunset.

for fun among us

 Our childhood was full of joy. Dancing, singing, swimming, making sand castles, running around and having countless memories of those days. It is an unforgettable childhood, but it will become a precious and beautiful treasure and be kept in your heart for a long time.

We had a very happy childhood and spent most of our time on the beach. The sea was part of our lives, and our space where we always played together. Our childhoods were pleasant and lively and not boring. How was your childhood?

Romantic

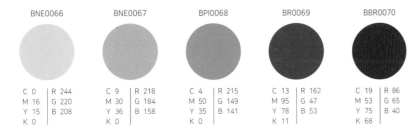

BNE0066	BNE0067	BPI0068	BR0069	BBR0070
C 0 R 244	C 9 R 218	C 4 R 215	C 13 R 162	C 19 R 86
M 16 G 220	M 30 G 184	M 50 G 149	M 95 G 47	M 53 G 65
Y 15 B 208	Y 36 B 158	Y 35 B 141	Y 78 B 53	Y 75 B 40
K 0	K 0	K 0	K 11	K 68

Color Palette - Light Pink Beige, Pink Beige, Coral Pink, Ruby Red, Deep Brown
핑크와 레드 조합은 따뜻하고 사랑스러우며 포근함마저 느껴집니다.
짙은 브라운을 포인트 색상으로 추가하면 고상하고 우아한 느낌이 더해집니다.

2 color combination

3 color combination

4 color combination

The language of love

There are not a few words that have the same as love. It would also be a rebuttal to the fact that love is so diverse and complex. Words similar to love will talk about the broad meaning of the concept of love, and at the same time will talk about the various connotations underlying it. Love is a kind of conceptual group. Love covers from human love to family love and love between men and women.

Someone beside you

As love is a complex human mind, it is bound to be accompanied by a sense of morality or ethics. The kindness of heart was also based on love. On the other hand, love is also a part of the heart that emphasizes faith, at least as much as religion.

That is why the discourse of love should cover philosophy, psychology, religious theory, ethics, art theory, and even political theory. This is because love is a human heart that embraces both true and good and beauty, but also meets practical utility. The true meaning of love is a heart that cares and exerts all its energy to save people and beings.

Type of love
Be more romantic

Fruition of love
Completion of life

Wedding

Marriage is based on a vow that the two will keep their love forever. Marriage is a promise that two people will form a family and love their spouses in any difficulties and do their best for them.

If I know what is love, because of you.

Love is the warmest, most desirable human relationship.
It is a movement of mind that values and wants to protect each other.

45

Lovely

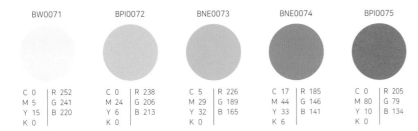

BW0071		BPI0072		BNE0073		BNE0074		BPI0075	
C 0	R 252	C 0	R 238	C 5	R 226	C 17	R 185	C 0	R 205
M 5	G 241	M 24	G 206	M 29	G 189	M 44	G 146	M 80	G 79
Y 15	B 220	Y 6	B 213	Y 32	B 165	Y 33	B 141	Y 10	B 134
K 0		K 0		K 0		K 6		K 0	

Color Palette - Ivory, Soft Pink, Pink Beige, Pink Cocoa, Hot Pink
핑크 계열 색상은 사랑스러운 이미지를 연출하기 쉬운 컬러입니다.
소프트한 브라운과 핑크 배색은 따뜻하고 귀여운 인상을 줄 수 있습니다.

2 color combination

3 color combination

4 color combination

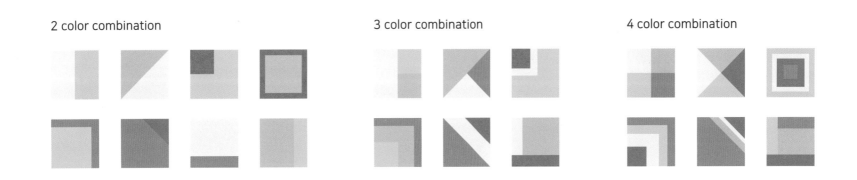

Companion Animals

In the past, animals that live with people were called 'pets' to mean that they are raised to entertain people. But these days, animals are called 'companion animals', meaning they are like friends and family, who live with people and give them a sense of psychological stability and intimacy. Taking care of pets creates a regular lifestyle, which also helps your health a lot.

The human & pet relationship

A friend or family who lives with people and gives them a sense of psychological stability and intimacy.

How to Take Care of them

There are many things to care about. It takes a little effort to get through the difficulties wisely and live with this faithful and cute friend. Above all, you have to understand them.

It is important to know what personality and habits Companion Animals have, how much exercise they need, what they can do well and what they can't do.

Living happily with your precious A friend or family

You need to know how to get close, how to be polite to others, how to take care of their health, and so on.

Calm

BNE0076	BNE0077	BNE0078	BGY0079	BBR0080
C 0 / R 249	C 0 / R 242	C 17 / R 203	C 53 / R 118	C 31 / R 78
M 9 / G 234	M 19 / G 213	M 31 / G 177	M 37 / G 125	M 56 / G 61
Y 10 / B 224	Y 23 / B 191	Y 36 / B 157	Y 24 / B 141	Y 64 / B 47
K 0	K 0	K 0	K 18	K 68

Color Palette - Light Peach, Soft Apricot, Dark Beige, Dark Blue Gray, Deep Brown

Calm은 명상을 하듯 차분하고 침착하며 변화가 없는 잔잔한 상태를 의미합니다.
밝은 톤 색상과 저채도의 중간 톤 색상을 조합하면 안정적이고 부드러운 이미지를 연출할 수 있습니다.

2 color combination   3 color combination   4 color combination

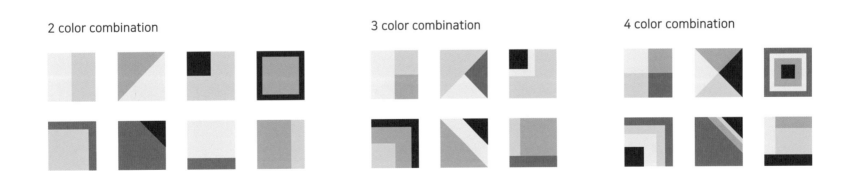

Why and for what do we meditate?

Meditation brings the effect of relaxation by relaxing the mind and relaxing the body. In particular, the unanalyzed posture of meditation helps to relax the mind.

01

Meditation brings various effects such as stress management, learning improvement, health improvement, performance improvement, drug addiction treatment, psychotherapy, religious spiritual development, habit correction, self-discipline. Meditation allows you to experience a setapa combined with a pleasant and relaxed mood and extreme awakening, and shows a stable pattern of brain activity.

To escape from the pain of the mind and return to a pure state of mind

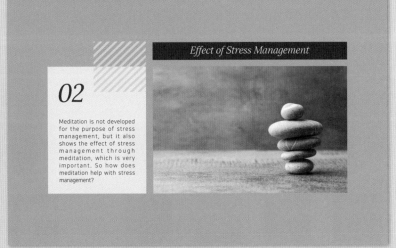

Effect of Stress Management

02

Meditation is not developed for the purpose of stress management, but it also shows the effect of stress management through meditation, which is very important. So how does meditation help with stress management?

Dark

BNE0081	BBR0082	BBR0083	BB0084	BBL0085

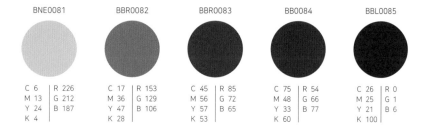

C 6 / R 226	C 17 / R 153	C 45 / R 85	C 75 / R 54	C 26 / R 0
M 13 / G 212	M 36 / G 129	M 56 / G 72	M 48 / G 66	M 25 / G 1
Y 24 / B 187	Y 47 / B 106	Y 57 / B 65	Y 33 / B 77	Y 21 / B 6
K 4	K 28	K 53	K 60	K 100

Color Palette - Beige, Milk Brown, Dark Brown, Dark Green Blue, Black
명도와 채도가 낮은 색상은 어둡고 무거우며, 강한 이미지를 표현합니다.
어두운 색상 그룹에 밝은 색상으로 포인트를 주면 대비가 강해져 지루하지 않은 배색이 됩니다.

2 color combination

3 color combination

4 color combination

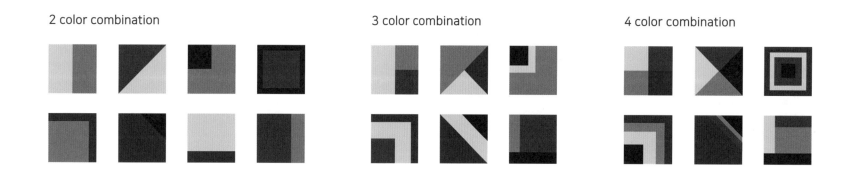

01

twinkle

Diamonds have excellent reflective and refractive properties, so if they are processed to make a few sides, they give off a colorful and beautiful light. Bright and colorful glitter shines more in the dark. Like the twinkling stars in the night sky, it symbolizes the inner hope of wandering and anxiety. Or, it is a tool that makes you a shining being and an object of desire to be recognized for its existence value.

02

*A state of
silence,
stillness,
quietness,
loneliness,
in the dark*

03

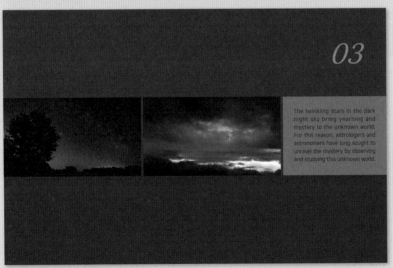

The twinkling stars in the dark night sky bring yearning and mystery to the unknown world. For this reason, astrologers and astronomers have long sought to unravel the mystery by observing and studying this unknown world.

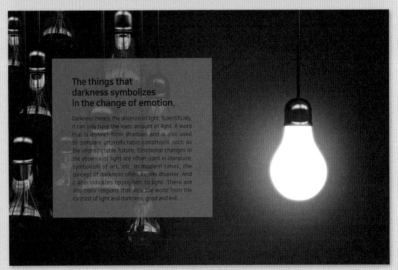

The things that darkness symbolizes in the change of emotion.

Darkness means the absence of light. Scientifically, it can only have the least amount of light. A word that is distinct from shadows and is also used to compare unpredictable conditions such as the unpredictable future. Emotional changes in the absence of light are often used in literature, symbolism of art, etc. In modern times, the concept of darkness often means disaster. And it also indicates opposition to light. There are also many religions that view the world from the contrast of light and darkness, good and evil.

POP

Playful

Picnic

Fruit Juice

Macaron

Party

Candy Jelly

Playful

BPI0086	BY0087	BPI0088	BG0089	BBR0090
C 3 R 238	C 0 R 251	C 0 R 214	C 59 R 140	C 26 R 98
M 15 G 222	M 7 G 226	M 62 G 125	M 0 G 188	M 82 G 52
Y 0 B 234	Y 80 B 81	Y 3 B 167	Y 84 B 89	Y 73 B 45
K 0	K 0	K 0	K 0	K 51

Color Palette - Light Pink, Canary Yellow, Rose Pink, Apple Green, Red brown
채도가 높은 색상은 밝고 경쾌한 인상을 줍니다.
중간 톤의 옐로, 핑크, 그린 배색을 활용하면 활기차고 즐거운 분위기를 연출할 수 있습니다.

2 color combination

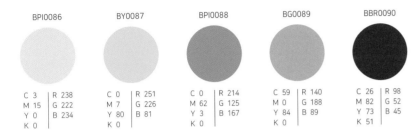

3 color combination

4 color combination

Paper art is more than just folding and creating all kinds of shapes without cutting or cutting a square sheet of paper. However, sometimes they put a house of scissors or paint, and sometimes they put gold and silver foil on it.

To Cook and Play
with Paper

Origami is more than just folding and creating all kinds of shapes without cutting or cutting a square sheet of paper.

THE ART AND PLAY OF FOLDING PAPER TO CREATE VARIOUS SHAPES SUCH AS BIRDS, CLOTHES, AND FLOWERS.

Origami is mainly used for educational purposes such as creativity, color sense, and handwork in kindergartens or elementary schools.

FRUIT, VEGETABLES, ANIMALS, COOKING, AND SO ON.
Cut and fold paper in various shapes to make the desired shape, decorate it, and use it as a play tool.

Paper

Paper folding can be divided into three areas: education, life, and creative origami. Educational origami aims to demonstrate creative and mathematical abilities by using origami. Household origami refers to making flowers, decorations, and household items for use in real life. The purpose of creative origami is to create a specific form in a new sequence.

How to do Paper folding

To enjoy origami, individuals can buy origami books or get information from the Internet. In order to teach origami for educational purposes, you need to learn about it separately.

55

Picnic

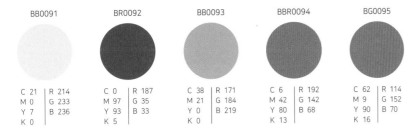

BB0091	BR0092	BB0093	BBR0094	BG0095
C 21 R 214	C 0 R 187	C 38 R 171	C 6 R 192	C 62 R 114
M 0 G 233	M 97 G 35	M 21 G 184	M 42 G 142	M 9 G 152
Y 7 B 236	Y 93 B 33	Y 0 B 219	Y 80 B 68	Y 90 B 70
K 0	K 5	K 0	K 13	K 16

Color Palette - Light Blue, Red, Pale Blue, Yellow Brown, Green

'Picnic'은 일상생활에서 벗어나 야외로 나가 산책이나 식사를 하면서 즐기는 일을 뜻합니다.
톤이 다른 레드, 블루, 브라운, 그린의 조합은 익숙함이 아닌 특별한 일상을 표현합니다.

2 color combination   3 color combination   4 color combination

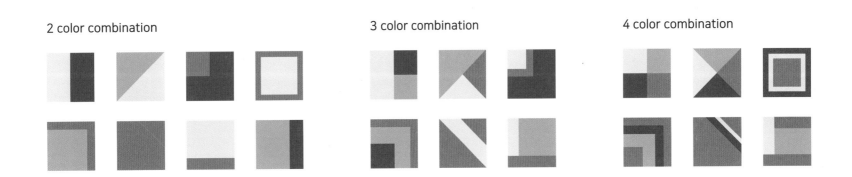

A fun and special day

Picnic refers to eating, drinking, chatting and enjoying food outdoors with friends in nature. Unlike hiking, a picnic is characterized by being free and comfortable regardless of schedule or course.

Let's go on a picnic there.

When you go on a picnic, you use nearby forests and natural parks that are not too far away. Spring flowers, hwajeon nori, summer water and fishing, and autumn foliage are also some of the picnic.

Fine weather clears the mind. I go on a picnic with a light heart to relax. I enjoy my own time in peace, eat leisurely and listen to music. The sky is clear, the leaves are fresh, and the sun is a dazzling season. Lying on the grass without thinking in a lively nature makes your body and mind heal, and it is a happy time.

Healing Time

Things you must prepare for a picnic

When going on a picnic, dress comfortably, and take things to rest and play outdoors, including simple food, fruits, and mats.

Fruit Juice

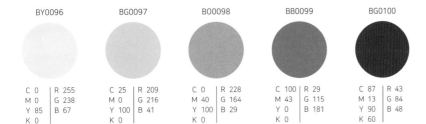

BY0096	BG0097	B00098	BB0099	BG0100
C 0 / R 255	C 25 / R 209	C 0 / R 228	C 100 / R 29	C 87 / R 43
M 0 / G 238	M 0 / G 216	M 40 / G 164	M 43 / G 115	M 13 / G 84
Y 85 / B 67	Y 100 / B 41	Y 100 / B 29	Y 0 / B 181	Y 90 / B 48
K 0	K 0	K 0	K 0	K 60

Color Palette - Lemon Yellow, Yellow Green, Citrus Orange, Strong Blue, Deep Green
명도와 채도가 높은 옐로, 그린, 오렌지 색상은 상큼한 시트러스 향을 떠올리게 합니다.
짙은 색상을 배색해 대비가 강해지면 맑고 투명한 이미지를 더할 수 있습니다.

2 color combination

3 color combination

4 color combination

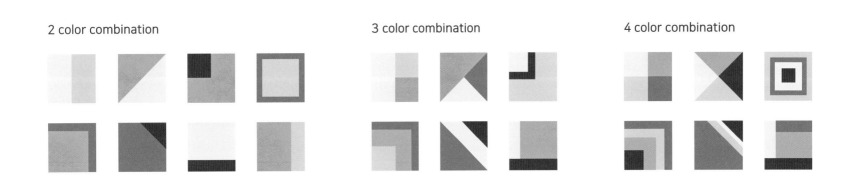

Making Fruit Juice

Apple juice, orange juice, lemon juice, grape juice, pineapple juice, tomato juice, carrot juice and so on.

Liquid juice squeezed from fruit.
Accurately refers to 100% natural fruit juice.

Fruit juice full of fresh lemon and orange

Fresh juice can make up for insufficient moisture and vitamin C, which is good not only for children but also for adults' snacks. Squeeze the juice of fruit or grind the whole fruit in a blender and drink it with juice as raw fruit.

It was only recently that fruit juice began to be sold as bottles or barrels. If you leave the juice intact, it ferments and becomes alcohol or vinegar, and when it boils, it loses its freshness. Grape juice only preserves freshness even when boiled, so it began to be sold as a bottle around the 19th century.

Citrus Aroma

Citrus means 'tangerine or its insides' in a dictionary sense. In wine terms, you can feel the aroma and flavor of oranges, lemons, lime and grapefruit. Refers to the basic aromas you can smell in the fresh, cool Dry White Wine.

Sweet, Fresh Fruitcake

Spread fruit jam on the bread sheet and stack it in three layers, and decorate the top with fresh fruit.

Macaron

BY0101	BG0102	B00103	BPI0104	BB0105

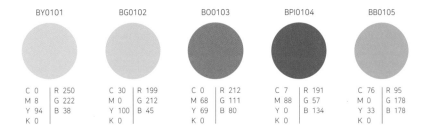

C 0	R 250	C 30	R 199	C 0	R 212	C 7	R 191	C 76	R 95
M 8	G 222	M 0	G 212	M 68	G 111	M 88	G 57	M 0	G 178
Y 94	B 38	Y 100	B 45	Y 69	B 80	Y 0	B 134	Y 33	B 178
K 0		K 0		K 0		K 0		K 0	

Color Palette - Yellow, Yellow Green, Orange, Hot Pink, Turquoise Blue
옐로, 그린, 오렌지, 핑크, 블루의 톤 인 톤 배색은 다양한 색상 변화를 보여줍니다.
각 색상의 개성이 모두 표현되므로 컬러풀한 이미지를 연출할 수 있습니다.

2 color combination   3 color combination   4 color combination

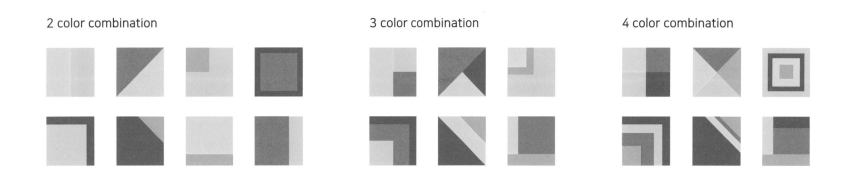

How to make round and colored macarons.

The ingredients are simple, but the recipe is difficult to make. When the egg whites and sugar are mixed together and bubbles are formed, the fine almond powder is mixed and baked in an oven. It is about 5cm in diameter and has a round shape. These days, it is usually made by applying cream between two macarons and putting them together. It is crispy on the outside and moist on the inside, and is usually flavored with coffee, chocolate, strawberry, hazelnut, pistachio, coconut, vanilla, etc.

What is your favorite flavor?

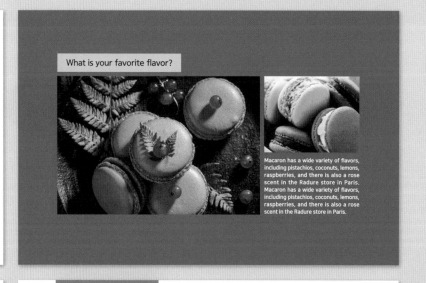

Macaron has a wide variety of flavors, including pistachios, coconuts, lemons, raspberries, and there is also a rose scent in the Radure store in Paris. Macaron has a wide variety of flavors, including pistachios, coconuts, lemons, raspberries, and there is also a rose scent in the Radure store in Paris.

HOW DO YOU PICK OUT MACARONS?

A well-made macaron has a smooth, glossy surface and a lace-like crease along its round rim, called 'feet of macarons.'

Party

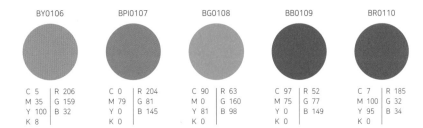

BY0106	BPI0107	BG0108	BB0109	BR0110
C 5 R 206	C 0 R 204	C 90 R 63	C 97 R 52	C 7 R 185
M 35 G 159	M 79 G 81	M 0 G 160	M 75 G 77	M 100 G 32
Y 100 B 32	Y 0 B 145	Y 81 B 98	Y 0 B 149	Y 95 B 34
K 8	K 0	K 0	K 0	K 0

Color Palette - Golden Yellow, Rose Pink, Kelly Green, Dark Royal Blue, Red
축하 및 기념을 위한 파티에서는 컬러풀한 풍선과 화려한 색종이 조각을 볼 수 있습니다.
채도가 높은 중간 톤 핑크, 그린, 블루, 레드의 톤 인 톤 배색은 화려하고 펑키한 분위기를 연출합니다.

2 color combination   3 color combination   4 color combination

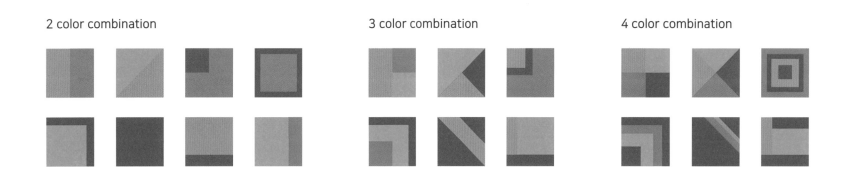

**TIME TO
ENJOY
THE PARTY**

A SPECTACULAR
FIREWORKS DISPLAY

A game in which various metallic compounds are added to gunpowder such as firecrackers to display colorful sparks. It can be seen as a way of conveying news from afar or as a festival-like event in that it makes a loud sound. In the early days, torches were used, and after the gunpowder was developed, this way became a fireworks display. There are various types of launches, production methods, night and day, and each has several chemical principles.

*Presents make
the party
more
enjoyable*

A gift from my heart is more powerful than anything else in the world. The gift also has the meaning of a beautiful evaluation of a person who did his best in life and worked hard in a given task.

When it's someone's birthday, people prepare birthday cakes and gifts, and have a birthday party.
Then put candles on the cake, and blow out the candlelight at once, and the birthday wishes come true.

Candy Jelly

BY0111	BPI0112	BO0113	BB0114	BPU0115

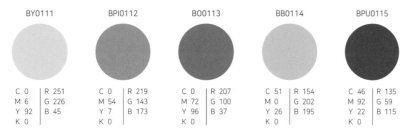

C 0	R 251	C 0	R 219	C 0	R 207	C 51	R 154	C 46	R 135
M 6	G 226	M 54	G 143	M 72	G 100	M 0	G 202	M 92	G 59
Y 92	B 45	Y 7	B 173	Y 96	B 37	Y 26	B 195	Y 22	B 115
K 0		K 0		K 0		K 0		K 0	

Color Palette - Yellow, Pink, Orange, Aqua Blue, Purple

달콤한 캔디와 젤리는 컬러풀한 색상으로 시선을 사로잡습니다.
비비드 톤의 활동적인 컬러 배색은 화려하고 경쾌하며 팝(POP)한 인상을 줍니다.

2 color combination

3 color combination

4 color combination

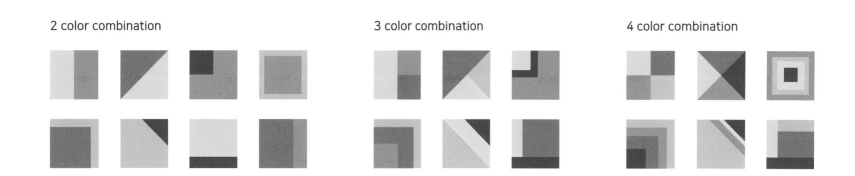

Lovely lollipop

Candy jelly

Candy is a kind of sweetened snack made by boiling sugar extracted from sugar cane with water and then hardening it. It has the effect of recovering from fatigue and feeling better.

Jelly is a food made by boiling water in fruit, squeezing juice, and boiling sugar in the pectin solution. The complete jelly shall be transparent and have a shiny gloss, the color shall be good and shall remain intact when taken out of the container, and shall have the flavor of the raw fruit.

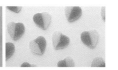

The euphoria of sweet candies

Candy is made by adding sugar as the main ingredient and other sugars, dairy products, fats, edible pigments, spices, fruits and nuts. Starch syrup is used for the purpose of preventing the re-determination of sugar and giving tissue viscosity to improve workmanship and luster.

Lollipop is one of the sugars made of boiled sugar, and is a form of a thick, elongated shape or various sizes of spherical egg candy attached to a stick so that it can be held and sucked by hand. Lollipop is available as a product of various colors and flavors, especially fruit-flavored.

STYLE

STYLE

Classic

Modern

Elegant

Chic

Luxurious

Noble

Urban

Ethnic

Retro

Classic

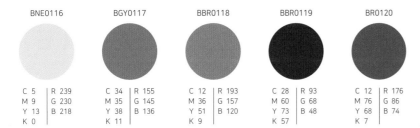

BNE0116	BGY0117	BBR0118	BBR0119	BR0120
C 5 R 239	C 34 R 155	C 12 R 193	C 28 R 93	C 12 R 176
M 9 G 230	M 35 G 145	M 36 G 157	M 60 G 68	M 76 G 86
Y 13 B 218	Y 38 B 136	Y 51 B 120	Y 73 B 48	Y 68 B 74
K 0	K 11	K 9	K 57	K 7

Color Palette - Light Beige, Warm Gray, Sandy Brown, Deep Brown, Dark Orange Red
Classic은 '고전적인, 유행을 안 타는'이라는 의미로 시대를 초월해 이어져 온 변하지 않는 스타일을 뜻합니다.
웜 톤의 베이지, 그레이, 브라운, 레드 배색은 따뜻하고 편안하지만 고풍스러운 이미지를 풍기기도 합니다.

2 color combination

3 color combination

4 color combination

**TIME TO
ENJOY
THE
CLASSIC**

NEOCLASSIC, MODERN INTERPRETATION OF CLASSIC

One of the western development based on the rare principles of ancient Greek and ancient Roman classics in architecture and design, For example, neoclassicism characterized by the French design of a period that lasted from the French Revolution to the 19th century, including the French house's regularity and the interior style of the Empire era.

Classical style that has continued beyond the ages.

Classic originally meant an old bibliography or record, but mainly refers to a literary or artistic work that is exemplary and highly regarded throughout the ages.

From the Byzantine period to the Renaissance period, Chandelier became an important role as one of the interior decoration points as well as for the original purpose of lighting.

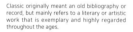

Modern

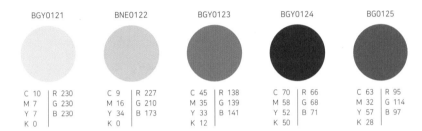

BGY0121	BNE0122	BGY0123	BGY0124	BG0125
C 10 R 230	C 9 R 227	C 45 R 138	C 70 R 66	C 63 R 95
M 7 G 230	M 16 G 210	M 35 G 139	M 58 G 68	M 32 G 114
Y 7 B 230	Y 34 B 173	Y 33 B 141	Y 52 B 71	Y 57 B 97
K 0	K 0	K 12	K 50	K 28

Color Palette - Light Pale Gray, Beige, Steel Gray, Dark Gray, Dark Green
Modern은 차갑고 간결하며, 현대적이고 도시적인 감각을 표현합니다.
무채색과 베이지, 그린을 조합하여 명도 대비를 강하게 주면 모던한 이미지를 연출할 수 있습니다.

2 color combination

3 color combination

4 color combination

MODERN STYLE INTERIOR AND ARCHITECTURE

Modern styles are also indispensable in the fields of architecture and interior design. Modern people feel comfort and visual beauty in simple and concisely organized geometric forms because they live in a large amount of fast-flowing information and complex and diverse environments.

01

The characteristic of modern images is that they pursue a rather cold, concise beauty and their urban sense stands out. Based on achromatic and cold colors, complementary colors with strong contrast in color and intensity are preferred, excluding softness and decorativity. The colors representing modern images are achromatic colors such as white, black, and gray, as well as turquoise and blue. Modern concepts have changed not only for commercial reasons that communicate with the modern public, but also for the goal of enriching human beings and their lives.

A MODERN STYLE SPACE WITH INTELLECTUAL BEAUTY AND SIMPLE

NATURAL MODERN STYLE

02

The style concept is the next most important thing to consi- der in interior design after its use and function that suits the lifestyle. The natural modern style interior is a style that adds warmth by creating natural furniture or fabric in a simple modern space.

Elegant

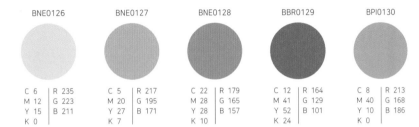

BNE0126		BNE0127		BNE0128		BBR0129		BPI0130	
C 6	R 235	C 5	R 217	C 22	R 179	C 12	R 164	C 8	R 213
M 12	G 223	M 20	G 195	M 28	G 165	M 41	G 129	M 40	G 168
Y 15	B 211	Y 27	B 171	Y 28	B 157	Y 52	B 101	Y 10	B 186
K 0		K 7		K 10		K 24		K 0	

Color Palette - Light Pink Beige, Pink Beige, Cocoa, Milk Brown, Pale Pink
Elegant는 기품이 서린 고급스러운 이미지를 연상하게 합니다.
베이지와 브라운 베이스에 핑크를 더해 우아하고 고상한 분위기를 표현합니다.

2 color combination   3 color combination   4 color combination

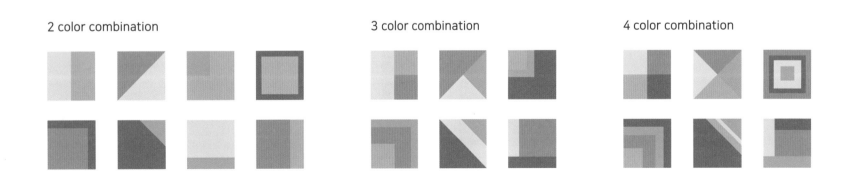

Why do women want to do elegant style?

The words 'Elegance' and 'Luxury' are used to express costumes or jewelry, but they also refer to people as 'Elegance'. In this respect, the meaning of Elegance does not seem to mean just the outward form. Also included are words or actions and the mood from etiquette.

Sophisticated, Elegant, and Luxurious

The dictionary definition of elegance is 'grace, nobility' which mainly means the outward appearance of a person. It also implies a noble character with classy words, courtesy, and good taste.

classy refinement

How and what will you make classy refinement?

An image that combines a sophisticated, elegant, and luxurious image gives people an attractive impression.

Chic

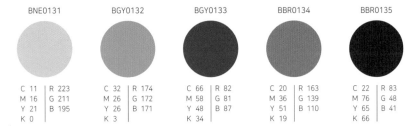

BNE0131	BGY0132	BGY0133	BBR0134	BBR0135

C 11	R 223	C 32	R 174	C 66	R 82	C 20	R 163	C 22	R 83
M 16	G 211	M 26	G 172	M 58	G 81	M 36	G 139	M 76	G 48
Y 21	B 195	Y 26	B 171	Y 48	B 87	Y 51	B 110	Y 65	B 41
K 0		K 3		K 34		K 19		K 66	

Color Palette - Beige, Gray, Dark Gray, Milk Brown, Chocolate Brown
Chic는 절제된 단순미와 고상하고 성숙한 지성미가 느껴지는 이미지를 뜻합니다.
무채색과 저채도, 저명도 색상 배색으로 세련되고 고급스러운 분위기를 연출합니다.

2 color combination

3 color combination

4 color combination

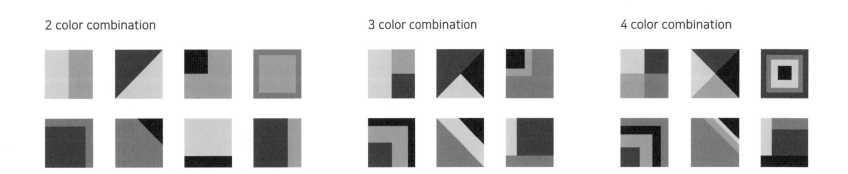

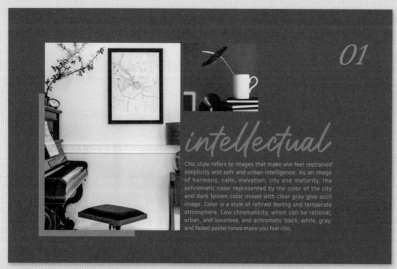

01

intellectual

Chic style refers to images that make one feel restrained simplicity and soft and urban intelligence. As an image of harmony, calm, elevation, city and maturity, the achromatic color represented by the color of the city and dark brown color mixed with clear gray give such image. Color is a style of refined feeling and temperate atmosphere. Low chromaticity, which can be rational, urban, and luxurious, and achromatic black, white, gray, and faded pastel tones make you feel chic.

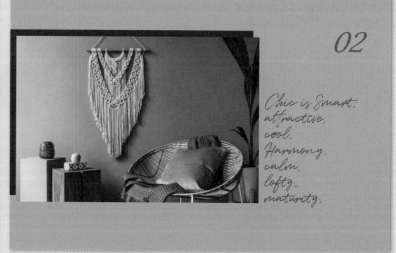

02

Chic is Smart, attractive, cool. Harmony, calm, lofty, maturity.

03

If you give black and gold points to low chroma pastel colors or light achromatic backgrounds, you can create a chic atmosphere by giving a modern, simple, elegant, and intelligent feeling due to the strong contrast of colors.

Chic is an image of restrained simplicity and soft, urban intelligence.

Chic is an image of harmony, calm, maturity and city, with achromatic color represented by the color of the city and a dark color mixed with clear and dark gray giving such an image. Color is a style of refined feeling and temperate atmosphere. Low chromaticity, which can represent rational, urban and intellectual luxury, black, white, gray and faded pastel tones and dark wine colors and gold combinations make you feel a chic image. With a modern and simple urban sense, it becomes a color that represents trends.

Luxurious

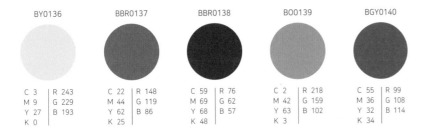

BY0136	BBR0137	BBR0138	BO0139	BGY0140
C 3 / R 243	C 22 / R 148	C 59 / R 76	C 2 / R 218	C 55 / R 99
M 9 / G 229	M 44 / G 119	M 69 / G 62	M 42 / G 159	M 36 / G 108
Y 27 / B 193	Y 62 / B 86	Y 68 / B 57	Y 63 / B 102	Y 32 / B 114
K 0	K 25	K 48	K 3	K 34

Color Palette - Cream Yellow, Peanut Brown, Dark Brown, Cream Orange, Dark Blue Gray
Luxurious는 고급스럽고 호화로운, 또는 사치스러운 이미지를 떠올리게 합니다.
진한 브라운을 베이스로 블루와 오렌지를 포인트로 배색하여 고급스럽고 화려한 분위기를 연출합니다.

2 color combination

3 color combination

4 color combination

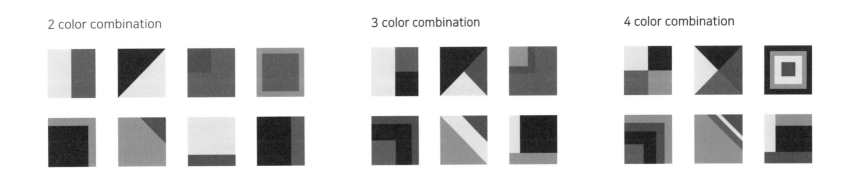

Luxury hotels are hotels that provide the highest level of facilities and services, providing the best customized services to customers. The hotel lobby is classy, and the rooms are equipped with high-quality furniture, excellent quality bedding and amenities. It has a restaurant with the best menu and best service, a banquet hall, and an international conference hall.

Luxurious and high class hotels

The brand of luxury goods is often named after the person who first designed the product or founded the company, and is usually priced much higher by the brand value than by the cost of the product.

LUXURY VILLAS, FINE FURNITURE, CARS, YACHTS, JEWELRY, CLOTHES, WATCHES AND SO ON.

Luxury goods are products that use expensive materials for the high-income consumer class and are produced in low-volume luxury.

SMALL LUXURIES LIKE CHOCOLATE AND FLOWERS

Small luxuries are part of daily life seeking small but easy-to-achieve happiness. They include chocolate or coffee, flowers, or small gifts consumed for emotional comfort or satisfaction.

Luxury goods

Luxury goods are mainly focused on goods such as furniture, automobiles, yachts, jewelry, clothing, watches, and service products such as luxury hotels and restaurants, including real estate such as mansions, luxury villas and luxury apartments. Luxury goods are products that use expensive materials and are made in small quantities luxurious.

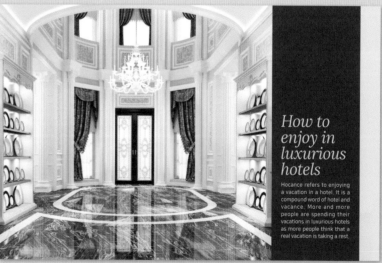

How to enjoy in luxurious hotels

Hocance refers to enjoying a vacation in a hotel. It is a compound word of hotel and vacance. More and more people are spending their vacations in luxurious hotels as more people think that a real vacation is taking a rest.

Noble

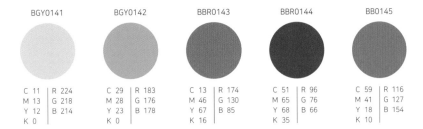

BGY0141	BGY0142	BBR0143	BBR0144	BB0145
C 11 R 224	C 29 R 183	C 13 R 174	C 51 R 96	C 59 R 116
M 13 G 218	M 28 G 176	M 46 G 130	M 65 G 76	M 41 G 127
Y 12 B 214	Y 23 B 178	Y 67 B 85	Y 68 B 66	Y 18 B 154
K 0	K 0	K 16	K 35	K 10

Color Palette - Light Beige Gray, Stone gray, Camel Brown, Dark Brown, Gray Blue
Noble은 고귀하며 기품과 위엄이 있는 이미지를 연상하게 합니다.
저채도의 그레이, 브라운, 블루 배색은 차분하고 우아하며 안정감 있는 이미지를 표현합니다.

2 color combination

3 color combination

4 color combination

Afternoon tea

The private and small tea-time habits enjoyed by guests who visited the Duchess became a trend among upper-class women at some point. Afternoon tea has become the most enjoyable social occasion for the Englishman. Tea-time entered the Victorian era and continued in drawing rooms and gardens. It is naturally produced with straight manners and refined topics while drinking snacks and tea.

The comfort of a sofa

If it is too soft, it is uncomfortable to sit and stand up, and it can strain your back because you can't support your weight evenly, so it's better to choose according to your purpose and mood rather than just looking for soft things.

The meaning of personal space

Personal space is classified into four categories depending on the closeness of the other person. It is divided into intimate space, personal space, social space, and public space and it is important to identify and understand the differences in each spatial concept. Also, the meaning of personal space varies depending on the culture.

Wallpaper and fabric that set the atmosphere

A cozy bedroom

It is fabric setting of wallpaper, curtains, and bedding that makes the bedroom cozy. The curtains in the bedroom should match the bedding, so it is better to plan together from the beginning.

Noble and elegant interior decorations

Hanging chandeliers and setting shirring curtains for the noble and elegant atmosphere is one of the ways.

Urban

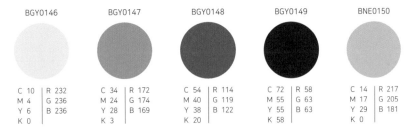

BGY0146	BGY0147	BGY0148	BGY0149	BNE0150
C 10 | R 232	C 34 | R 172	C 54 | R 114	C 72 | R 58	C 14 | R 217
M 4 | G 236	M 24 | G 174	M 40 | G 119	M 55 | G 63	M 17 | G 205
Y 6 | B 236	Y 28 | B 169	Y 38 | B 122	Y 55 | B 63	Y 29 | B 181
K 0	K 3	K 20	K 58	K 0

Color Palette - Light Pale Gray, Light Steel Gray, Steel Gray, Dark Gray, Beige
Urban은 '도시의, 도회의'라는 뜻으로, 도시 특유의 감각이나 라이프스타일을 의미합니다.
무채색의 톤 온 톤 배색을 베이스로 웜 톤의 포인트 컬러를 넣어 심플하고 세련된 감각을 표현합니다.

2 color combination

3 color combination

4 color combination

How to do Urban Style Interior

A CITY SPECIFIC SENSE OR LIFESTYLE

The city is the center of social, economic, and political activities, where thousands and tens of thousands of people live in groups, and houses are concentrated and transportation routes are concentrated. Today, the whole world is in an era of rapid urbanization and urban civilization.

Sociologists use the meaning of a city as a term that encompasses the environment built within the urban dwellings. Urban society, urban life, and urbanization refer to social life in the city. Cities have their own unique and distinct ways of life and the ability to produce socio-cultural changes.

TIPS FOR A REFINED AND SENSUOUS INTERIOR DESIGN

WHAT AND HOW WILL YOU DO IT

In the past, there was a strong tendency to identify the interior of a building in the sense of simply embedding it by separating it from the main body of the structure. However, in the 20th century, the idea that the interior should be a functional and harmonious space in real life led to the need for technology as a design rather than decoration.

URBAN STYLE
INTERIOR

Components of the interior include fixed sections of ceilings, floors, walls, and various structures, as well as operating sections of furniture, rugs, curtains, etc., and the interior decoration should consist of design styles taking into account both lighting and color, in addition to their layout.

Ethnic

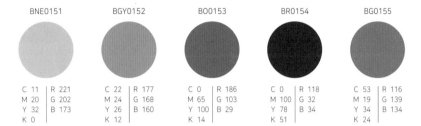

BNE0151	BGY0152	BO0153	BR0154	BG0155
C 11　R 221	C 22　R 177	C 0　R 186	C 0　R 118	C 53　R 116
M 20　G 202	M 24　G 168	M 65　G 103	M 100　G 32	M 19　G 139
Y 32　B 173	Y 26　B 160	Y 100　B 29	Y 78　B 34	Y 34　B 134
K 0	K 12	K 14	K 51	K 24

Color Palette - Deige, Warm Gray, Burnt Orange, Dark Red, Teal Green
Ethnic은 아프리카, 중남미, 몽골 등의 민족 색채가 짙은 스타일을 뜻하며
도시와 다른 색과 감성을 표현합니다.
오렌지, 레드, 그린을 배색하여 이국적이고 화려하면서 활력 있는 분위기를 연출합니다.

2 color combination

3 color combination

4 color combination

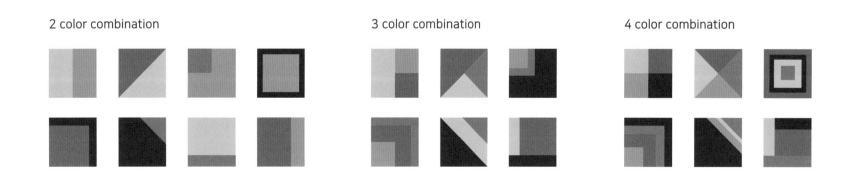

ethnic style

Ethnic refers to the traditional image of a species different from modern Western culture. Specifically, it refers to the traditional style of certain ethnic groups, including Africa, Junggeun-dong, Latin America, Central Asia and Mongolia. It aims to find vitality in urban life by adding unique colors, materials, and handicrafts.

Ethnic printes for the interior point

Among the natural images, the proportion of products that have attracted animals as motifs is increasing. The pattern or design itself is modeled after a particular animal, and the image that was used only as a point due to its strong image is sometimes used as a representative image of space. In particular, the ethnic style is characterized by adding modern elements to the wild feeling or intense and lively image given by Africa to create a feel like an art work.

Having Only sweet dreams

Dreamcatcher is a ring shaped hand-made ornament the Native Americans believed to filter out nightmares and allow only good dreams. A round frame of a willow-tree loop is woven like a spider's web, and underneath the ring is decorated with feathers and beads. Here, feathers make you have a good dream, and spider webs filter out nightmares.

Patterns of geometric or ethnic patterns leaves a splendid and strong impression depending on the color.
A strong pattern is difficult to match with other interior decorations, but if well arranged, it can produce a unique style.

Retro

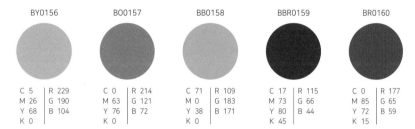

BY0156	B00157	BB0158	BBR0159	BR0160
C 5 / R 229	C 0 / R 214	C 71 / R 109	C 17 / R 115	C 0 / R 177
M 26 / G 190	M 63 / G 121	M 0 / G 183	M 73 / G 66	M 85 / G 65
Y 68 / B 104	Y 76 / B 72	Y 38 / B 171	Y 80 / B 44	Y 72 / B 59
K 0	K 0	K 0	K 45	K 15

Color Palette - Mellow Yellow, Orange, Turquoise Blue, Red Brown, Orange Red

Retro는 '복고주의, 복고풍'을 의미하며, 과거의 유행을 꺼내 향수를 느끼게 하는 양식을 뜻합니다.
귀엽고 발랄한 옐로, 오렌지, 블루의 중간 톤 배색에 브라운과 레드를 더하여 복고 무드를 표현합니다.

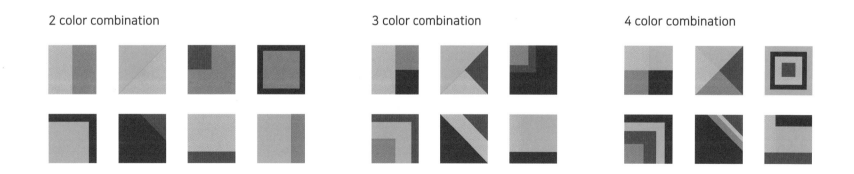

2 color combination

3 color combination

4 color combination

Retrospect

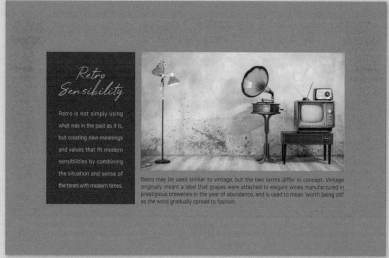

Retro Sensibility

Retro is not simply using what was in the past as it is, but creating new meanings and values that fit modern sensibilities by combining the situation and sense of the times with modern times.

Retro may be used similar to vintage, but the two terms differ in concept. Vintage originally meant a label that grapes were attached to elegant wines manufactured in prestigious breweries in the year of abundance, and is used to mean 'worth being old' as the word gradually spread to fashion.

Retro is nostalgia for the past

Retro is the abbreviation of the English word 'Retrospect', which means 'memory', and refers to a tendency to copy past memories. In other words, what existed or was popular in the past is the resurgence of what is now, and is mainly used in fashion, interior design, and popular music.

Retro refers to taking back what was popular in the past, missing the past, and feeling the nostalgia. Newtro is a newly coined term combining New and Retro, which refers to a tendency to enjoy retro. Cafes and restaurants that are decorated with items and props that seem to have turned back time have recently become popular.

OVERSEAS

London

New York

Italy

Greece

Paris

Scandinavia

Mexico

Africa

India

China

Japan

London

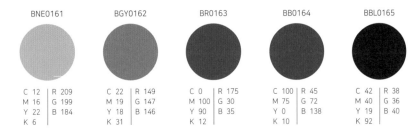

BNE0161	BGY0162	BR0163	BB0164	BBL0165
C 12 R 209	C 22 R 149	C 0 R 175	C 100 R 45	C 42 R 38
M 16 G 199	M 19 G 147	M 100 G 30	M 75 G 72	M 40 G 36
Y 22 B 184	Y 18 B 146	Y 90 B 35	Y 0 B 138	Y 19 B 40
K 6	K 31	K 12	K 10	K 92

Color Palette - Gray Beige, Gray, Red, Dark Royal Blue, Black

런던 하면 빨간 버스와 전화 부스, 그리고 흐린 날씨의 회색빛 하늘이 연상됩니다.
유니언잭에 사용한 레드와 블루를 중심으로 그레이 톤을 배색하면 런던의 분위기를 연출할 수 있습니다.

2 color combination

3 color combination

4 color combination

London is
a Good Place
to Travel

A GOOD WAY TO TRAVEL LONDON

The red double-decker bus is a symbol and a specialty of London. In particular, the front seats on the second floor are always popular among travelers as they are a good place to enjoy the view of London. If you go to the traffic information center, you can get a bus route map.

London Underground is the oldest urban railway in the world and operates in the surrounding areas such as Great Britain's Greater London, Essex, Hartfordshire, and Buckinghamshire. The London Underground has 270 stations and has the largest number of passengers per station.

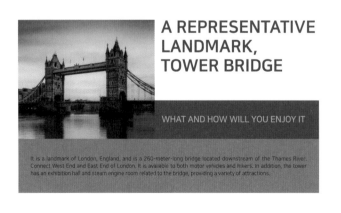

A REPRESENTATIVE LANDMARK, TOWER BRIDGE

WHAT AND HOW WILL YOU ENJOY IT

It is a landmark of London, England, and is a 260-meter-long bridge located downstream of the Thames River. Connect West End and East End of London. It is available to both motor vehicles and hikers. In addition, the tower has an exhibition hall and steam engine room related to the bridge, providing a variety of attractions.

TRAVELING LONDON

London is the capital of England and the birthplace of modern democracy. Developed along the Thames, London is one of the world's leading centers in arts, commerce, education, entertainment, fashion, health care, media and professional services. In particular, the financial industry is unrivaled.

New York

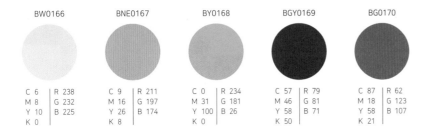

BW0166	BNE0167	BY0168	BGY0169	BG0170
C 6 | R 238	C 9 | R 211	C 0 | R 234	C 57 | R 79	C 87 | R 62
M 8 | G 232	M 16 | G 197	M 31 | G 181	M 46 | G 81	M 18 | G 123
Y 10 | B 225	Y 26 | B 174	Y 100 | B 26	Y 58 | B 71	Y 58 | B 107
K 0	K 8	K 0	K 50	K 21

Color Palette - Sand White, Sand Beige, Honey Yellow, Dark Gray, Peacock Green

뉴욕의 빌딩 숲속에 활력을 주는 노란 택시와 초록 표지판은 도시의 이미지를 상징합니다.
도시의 콘크리트를 연상시키는 베이지와 그레이를 베이스로
옐로, 그린으로 포인트를 주면 생동감이 살아납니다.

2 color combination

3 color combination

4 color combination

Statue of Liberty

The statue was erected in Liberty Island at the entrance of the Hudson River to New York Harbor, and was presented by France in 1886 to commemorate the 100th anniversary of American independence. The huge torch-bearer statue is officially named "Liberty Enlightening the World," but it is commonly known as the Statue of Liberty. It began to be built in 1875, completed in 1884, and was briefly stopped in Paris, France, before being transported to the United States by ship in 1885, and erected in its current location in 1886.

Manhattan and Brooklyn

A bridge connecting Manhattan and Brooklyn. It is considered the most beautiful bridge in New York. At the time of its opening, it attracted attention as the longest bridge in the world. It is the first suspension bridge to use iron cables and is highly regarded for its urban design.

BROOKLYN BRIDGE

The Brooklyn Bridge can be crossed on foot, with the first floor being a driveway and the second floor being a sidewalk. In the middle of the bridge is the 84-meter-high Brooklyn Tower, built in Gothic style. The sidewalk is divided into a bicycle road on the left and a pedestrian road on the right, with pictures on the floor to distinguish them. It takes about an hour to walk from end to end of the bridge.

A Symbol of New York, Empire State Building

It has long been loved by many people as a symbol of New York since it was built in 1931. It was the tallest building in the world when it was first completed with a height of 381 meters and 102 stories. The 67-meter-high television broadcasting antenna was additionally installed in 1950.

THE LARGEST CITY IN THE UNITED STATES.

New York is the center of commerce, finance and trade in the United States. Many universities, research institutes, museums, theaters, movie theaters, etc. occupy an important position as the center of American culture.

Italy

BB0171	BB0172	BO0173	BG0174	BR0175

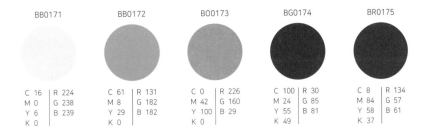

C 16	R 224	C 61	R 131
M 0	G 238	M 8	G 182
Y 6	B 239	Y 29	B 182
K 0		K 0	

C 0	R 226	C 100	R 30
M 42	G 160	M 24	G 85
Y 100	B 29	Y 55	B 81
K 0		K 49	

C 8	R 134
M 84	G 57
Y 58	B 61
K 37	

Color Palette - Light Blue, Peacock Blue, Citrus Orange, Dark Peacock Green, Burgundy Red
Italy에서 블루는 지중해를, 레드와 옐로는 열정과 활기를 상징합니다.
밝은 블루와 짙은 그린, 레드 컬러 베이스에 옐로를 포인트로 사용하여 이탈리아의 감성을 연출합니다.

2 color combination 3 color combination 4 color combination

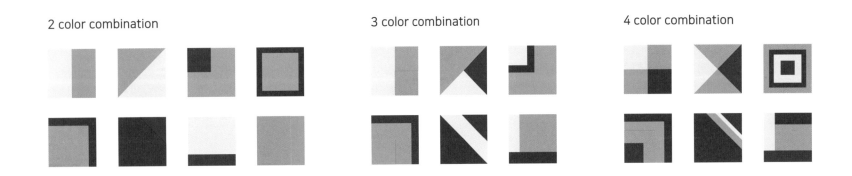

Venice, a city of water developed on the lagoon leading to the sea, is a historic port city and is a world-famous tourist destination. Located at the end of the Adriatic Sea east of the Italian Peninsula, it consists of about 120 small islands and is connected by 150 canals.

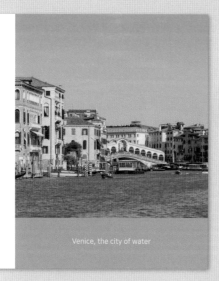

Venice, the city of water

Pasta is Italy's signature dish, mainly made by boiling flour dough in salt water, and there are various kinds.

TAGLIATELLE, LASAGNETTE, MAFALDINE, FETTUCCINE, SPAGHETTI, PENNE LISCE, AND TORTIGLIONI.

Pasta means 'paste, dough, batter' in Italian. In the past, it was called 'pasta alimentare' meaning a dough that can be absorbed from the body and replenished with nutrients.

ONE OF THE SEVEN WONDERS OF THE WORLD.

Piazza del Duomo, which houses the Leaning Tower of Pisa, as well as cathedrals, baptisms, and charnel houses, was listed as a UNESCO World Heritage Site in 1987.

Leaning Tower of Pisa

It is on the east side of the Pisa Cathedral. It is a cylindrical eight-story pagoda made of white marble, with a maximum height of 58.36 meters and estimated to weigh 14,453 tons. Construction began in 1173 and was carried out for about 200 years on three occasions from 1372 to 1372. After the first construction between 1173 and 1178, an imbalance in ground soil was discovered.

How to enjoy traveling Italy

Italy has a unique food culture in each region. In the northern part of Milan and Venice, the rice production is high and dairy products such as cheese and butter are abundant, so dishes such as risotto have developed.

Greece

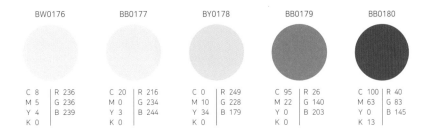

BW0176	BB0177	BY0178	BB0179	BB0180
C 8 R 236	C 20 R 216	C 0 R 249	C 95 R 26	C 100 R 40
M 5 G 236	M 0 G 234	M 10 G 228	M 22 G 140	M 63 G 83
Y 4 B 239	Y 3 B 244	Y 34 B 179	Y 0 B 203	Y 0 B 145
K 0	K 0	K 0	K 0	K 13

Color Palette - Cloudy White, Light Blue, Cream Yellow, Strong Blue, Deep Blue
하얀 골목, 파란 교회당, 짙고 푸른 바다가 있는 산토리니는 그리스의 상징입니다.
옅은 그레이와 청량감 있는 블루로 대비를 심화해 맑고 시원한 이미지를 강조합니다.

2 color combination

3 color combination

4 color combination

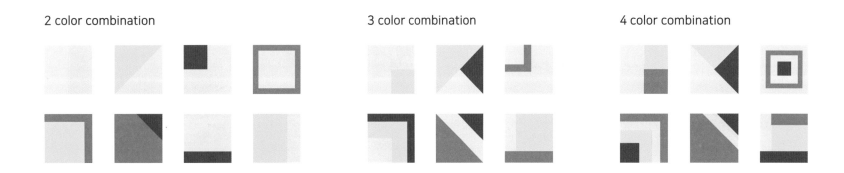

Traveling Greece with a Beautiful Blue Ocean

Greece, a country of gods surrounded by the Mediterranean Sea to the south and the Aegean Sea to the east.

Countless tourists are visiting Greece to find the roots of European culture and art.
Greece is like a museum as a whole country.

A VILLAGE COLORED WITH BLUE & WHITE

In the novel [Zorba the Greek], 'Someone who has the luck to travel to the Aegean Sea before they die has Blessed' has a content. In the novel, the islands of the Aegean Sea are the medium that connects reality to the dream world.

Santorini is an 'island washed by the light.' Even the red-bugenbilea, decorated with white alleys, blue churches, and fences, is clear. The coastal village I saw in the postcard is more beautiful and intense when you encounter reality. Santorini, a coveted island in the Aegean Sea, had such a dazzling and special landscape.

REGARD COOKING AS ART

It's not fancy, but it only uses fresh things about the ingredients. Fresh caught fruits, vegetables, and fish are also used as ingredients. Salad with vegetables is a must-eat course for Greeks, which consumes a lot of tomatoes, eggplants, and cucumbers, as well as olives.

Santorini Island

Since the 1980s, it has become famous as a venue for weddings or honeymoon trips, and it is estimated that about 500 weddings will be held annually.

Paris

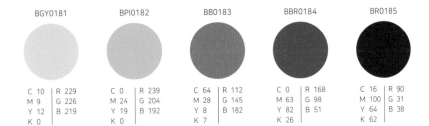

BGY0181	BPI0182	BB0183	BBR0184	BR0185
C 10 R 229	C 0 R 239	C 64 R 112	C 0 R 168	C 16 R 90
M 9 G 226	M 24 G 204	M 28 G 145	M 63 G 98	M 100 G 31
Y 12 B 219	Y 19 B 192	Y 8 B 182	Y 82 B 51	Y 64 B 38
K 0	K 0	K 7	K 26	K 62

Color Palette - Light Beige Gray, Soft Peach Pink, Ocean Blue, Orange Brown, Dark Red
영감을 북돋아 주는 핑크빛 구름과 노을에 물든 에펠탑. 늦은 오후의 파리에는 낭만이 가득합니다.
핑크, 블루, 브라운을 조합한 배색은 낭만적인 분위기를 연출하는 데 어울립니다.

2 color combination

3 color combination

4 color combination

Why do travelers Want to go to Paris

Paris, the capital of France and the representative city of Europe. From representative buildings such as the Eiffel Tower, Arc de Triomphe, Notre Dame Cathedral, and Versailles Palace, to the Orche Museum and the Louvre Museum, Paris has many landmarks and works of art that are hard to look around on a short schedule. Like France, which is called a gourmet country, there are many famous restaurants in Paris that attract gourmets such as escargot, foie gras, baguettes, and crepes.

Le dessert termine les repas

It is no exaggeration to say that the French ate all the long course meals above to eat dessert. From very sweet cakes to chocolate mousse, various desserts are developed.

How to See Montmartre

Eiffel Tower, the symbol of Paris

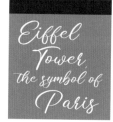

The Eiffel Tower is loved as a representative landmark of Paris and was listed as a World Heritage Site in 1991.

Scandinavia

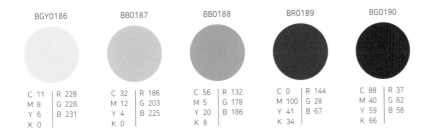

BGY0186	BB0187	BB0188	BR0189	BG0190
C 11 R 228	C 32 R 186	C 56 R 132	C 0 R 144	C 88 R 37
M 8 G 228	M 12 G 203	M 5 G 178	M 100 G 28	M 40 G 62
Y 6 B 231	Y 4 B 225	Y 20 B 186	Y 41 B 67	Y 59 B 58
K 0	K 0	K 8	K 34	K 66

Color Palette - Light Pale Gray, Light Pale Blue, Peacock Blue, Raspberry Red, Black Green
북유럽의 도시는 하얀 눈이 쌓인 겨울의 이미지가 강하게 떠오릅니다.
쿨 톤의 그레이, 블루, 레드, 그린 조합으로 해가 진 후 차가운 공기가 감싸는 북유럽의 도시를 표현합니다.

2 color combination

3 color combination

4 color combination

SCANDINAVIA, FIVE NORDIC COUNTRIES

Scandinavia means the history and region of the Scandinavian Peninsula in the Northern European peninsula. Basically, it is the three countries of Denmark, Norway, and Sweden, but it extends to Finland and Iceland due to the similarity of politics, economy, society and culture.

01

Reindeer are mammals of the deer family. It is the only kind of deer that has been domesticated. According to Santa Claus legend, he can fly in the sky and is famous for dragging Santa's sleigh. Living in the tundra area around the North Pole and moving to the southern forest in winter, it is rare to travel south of 60° north. Today, Eskimos live with reindeer and use them to pull sleds. Used as meat and wet food and leather is widely used as daily necessities such as clothing, tents, shoes and gloves.

HOW TO MEET SANTA CLAUS BEFORE CHRISTMAS COMES

SCANDINAVIAN CUISINE

02

Scandinavian cuisine has a simple recipe. Fish, meat and potatoes are the main food ingredients, and the use of spices is small. The signature dish, Gravlax, is made from processed salmon by dipping it in salt, sugar, and dill and pickled.

Mexico

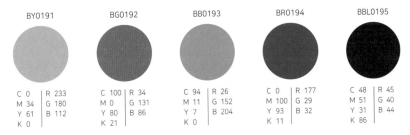

BY0191	BG0192	BB0193	BR0194	BBL0195
C 0 R 233	C 100 R 34	C 94 R 26	C 0 R 177	C 48 R 45
M 34 G 180	M 0 G 131	M 11 G 152	M 100 G 29	M 51 G 40
Y 61 B 112	Y 80 B 86	Y 7 B 204	Y 93 B 32	Y 31 B 44
K 0	K 21	K 0	K 11	K 86

Color Palette - Cream Orange, Deep Apple Green, Deep Sky Blue, Red, Black

타코, 살사, 테킬라의 나라 멕시코는 강렬하고 열정이 넘칩니다.
비비드 톤의 그린, 블루, 레드에 블랙을 더하여 멕시코의 열정적인 분위기를 연출합니다.

2 color combination   3 color combination   4 color combination

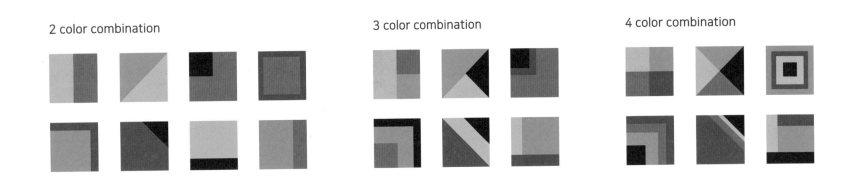

01

Mexico

Anyone interested in Mexican art, which reveals the beauty and rich emotions of red and blue primary colors, will naturally come to mind the best painters produced by Mexico, "Frida Kalla" and "Dego Rivera." Where can you feel the works of this century's artist couple who grew and worked based on Mexico City? If you follow their colorful and unique lives around Mexico City, you will fall in love with Mexican art.

02

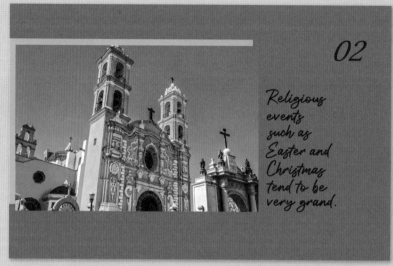

Religious events such as Easter and Christmas tend to be very grand.

03

Mexico is a country where the Maya, Aztec, Theotiouacan and Toltec civilizations blossomed splendidly, and the whole country is like a museum. It is a place with beautiful natural environment and cultural heritage like jewelry.

A colorful dish that combines ancient civilization with Spanish culture.

Taco is eaten with salsa sauce by putting chopped meat, vegetables and cheese on a round, thin tortilla made of flour or cornmeal. There must be three kinds of salsa sauce. Salsa verde, a sauce made by grinding green hot pepper Havana, and salsa mehikana with tomato and onion sauce and cilantro are typical. Guacamole is another sauce, which is eaten in pieces of fried tortilla called Totopo, similar to corn chips. 'Gwaka' comes from 'Aguacate', which means avocado, and 'Mole' means 'source' in a native Mexican language.

Africa

BNE0196	BY0197	BBR0198	BR0199	BBL0200

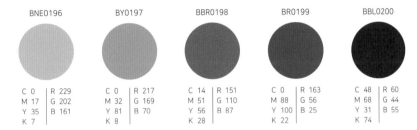

C 0 / R 229	C 0 / R 217	C 14 / R 151	C 0 / R 163	C 48 / R 60
M 17 / G 202	M 32 / G 169	M 51 / G 110	M 88 / G 56	M 68 / G 44
Y 35 / B 161	Y 81 / B 70	Y 56 / B 87	Y 100 / B 25	Y 31 / B 55
K 7	K 8	K 28	K 22	K 74

Color Palette - Yellow Beige, Mustard Yellow, Light Chocolate Brown, Dark Orange Red, Black
풍부한 자원이 가득한 아프리카 대륙은 광활하지만 적도를 품고 있어 무더운 지역이 많습니다.
이글거리는 열기와 토양을 상징하는 옐로, 브라운, 레드를 배색하여 아프리카를 표현합니다.

2 color combination

3 color combination

4 color combination

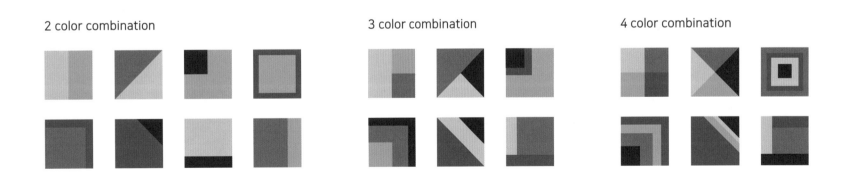

Africa is A Good Place To See Wild Animals

African zebras, foxes, cheetahs

Zebras have beautiful horizontal stripes on their bodies, and their body lengths vary depending on the type of body, have a larger head than the body, and have long fur only at the tip of the tail. Hoofs are wider than donkeys and narrower than horses. The ear is about the middle of a donkey and a horse.

The cheetah is a type of leopard belonging to the cat family, whose body is thin and long and legs make it the fastest way to run among mammals. The yellow body has a round black pattern that resembles a leopard, but the black spot of the leopard is ring-shaped, compared to the round one of cheetahs.

WHY IS FLAMINGOS STANDING ON ONE LEG?

Flamingos live in lakes, wetlands, and the sea all their lives.

Flamingos usually stand on one leg, while the other is under the body. The reason for this action is not fully known. One theory is to maintain body temperature, given that flamingos often stay in the water. Another theory is that if you stand on one leg and balance it, you can reduce the use of energy to build muscles.

TRAVELING AFRICA

Safari is one of the ways to travel in Africa. It also means to see animals in safari parks by car. Safari provides an opportunity to reflect on the contradictions of destruction and loss of value that human-oriented order inevitably causes. Safari can reflect on what values and the world human beings really need to pursue.

India

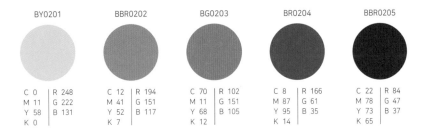

BY0201		BBR0202		BG0203		BR0204		BBR0205	
C 0	R 248	C 12	R 194	C 70	R 102	C 8	R 166	C 22	R 84
M 11	G 222	M 41	G 151	M 11	G 151	M 87	G 61	M 78	G 47
Y 58	B 131	Y 52	B 117	Y 68	B 105	Y 95	B 35	Y 73	B 37
K 0		K 7		K 12		K 14		K 65	

Color Palette - Light Mellow Yellow, Sandy Brown, Kelly Green, Dark Orange Red, Chocolate Brown
다양한 종교와 문화의 나라 인도는 향신료와 홍차의 나라로 알려져 있기도 합니다.
커리와 다즐링이 떠오르는 옐로, 브라운, 레드와 국기의 그린 컬러를 조합하여 인도 분위기를 연출합니다.

2 color combination

3 color combination

4 color combination

Islamic culture

The study of the Islamic world is closely related to religion because of the characteristics of Islamic culture, which is generally a religion and a unity of life. Linguistics to teach the immigrants Arabic and law and theology for the interpretation of the Quran formed the center of learning. In addition, many history books have been compiled in efforts to find the track record of Muhammad and early Muslims.

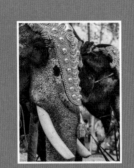

Indian food
made with mixed spices

Indian curry

Curry is a generic term for a dish made with masala, an Indian blend of spices. Curry has no set recipe, and the taste, aroma, and spiciness of Curry depends on which combination of maesala is used. In India, curry is believed to have been eaten since ancient times.

Curry can be divided into soupy wet curries and dry curries with little soup, depending on the shape. Curry makes soup with yogurt, coconut milk, ground dal, and broth; Dry curry is made by cooking with a small amount of soup so that spices are soaked in the ingredients, and then boiling it down to make sure that there is little soup left.

UNESCO
World Heritage

The Taj Mahal

Built by Shah Jahan, the emperor of the Mughal Empire, in memory of his beloved wife, Taj Mahal is one of India's finest Islamic art works and one of the greatest cultural heritages of the world.

The country of various religions and cultures

Hinduism, a religion unique to India, is deeply rooted in the lives of Indians, and when you travel to India, you can see Hindu temples everywhere. You can also experience the beauty of Buddhism by visiting places where Buddha was born and places where Buddha was enlightened.

China

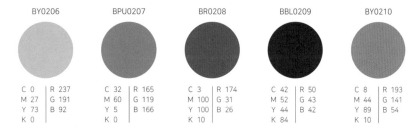

BY0206	BPU0207	BR0208	BBL0209	BY0210
C 0 / R 237	C 32 / R 165	C 3 / R 174	C 42 / R 50	C 8 / R 193
M 27 / G 191	M 60 / G 119	M 100 / G 31	M 52 / G 43	M 44 / G 141
Y 73 / B 92	Y 5 / B 166	Y 100 / B 26	Y 44 / B 42	Y 89 / B 54
K 0	K 0	K 10	K 84	K 10

Color Palette - Light Orange Yellow, Lilac Purple, Red, Black, Golden Yellow
세계 최대 인구와 광대한 국토를 가진 중국의 상징 컬러는 레드와 골든 옐로입니다.
레드, 옐로를 베이스로 퍼플과 블랙으로 포인트를 주면 화려하고 강인한 인상을 줄 수 있습니다.

2 color combination   3 color combination   4 color combination

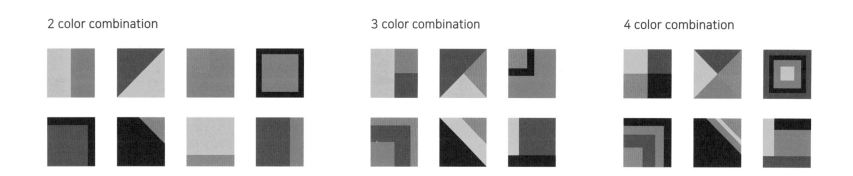

Chinese people and culture

China is made up of 56 ethnic groups, with more than 93 percent of the Han Chinese belonging to the Mongolians.

The reason for the worship of red in the daily lives of the Chinese people stems from their attachment to the yellow soil, which is called the birth of life.

The four major regional cuisine of China

China has a wide land area, so it has different characteristics in climate and products of each province. As a result, various factors such as economy, geography, society, and culture worked to form the four major dishes.

The Huanghe River Basin and the North are represented by Beijing cuisine, the lower reaches of the Yangtze River are represented by Shanghai cuisine, the upper middle reaches of the Yangtze River are represented by Sichuan cuisine and the lower reaches of the Zhu River are represented by Guangdong cuisine.

China & tea

Chinese tea has an immeasurable variety in the number of tea products. A good tea refers to a tea with a high reputation in the consumer market, with good teas mainly set by major tea producing areas, and also divided into historical good teas, traditional good teas and newly developed good teas.

Traditional chinese architecture

Traditional Chinese architectural technology is the product of history created by the Chinese, interacting with certain natural environments, building materials, technology levels and social ideologies.

Japan

BNE0211	BPI0212	BR0213	BB0214	BBR0215
C 7 R 233	C 0 R 232	C 9 R 157	C 70 R 104	C 34 R 79
M 12 G 222	M 34 G 184	M 100 G 37	M 38 G 137	M 48 G 68
Y 17 B 207	Y 20 B 179	Y 89 B 38	Y 5 B 186	Y 78 B 42
K 0	K 0	K 17	K 0	K 66

Color Palette - Light Beige, Peach Pink, Ruby Red, Sea Blue, Dark Khaki Brown
바다에 둘러싸인 섬나라 일본은 푸른 바다와 핑크빛 벚꽃, 그리고 검은 지붕을 떠올리게 합니다.
국기의 레드와 벚꽃의 핑크를 베이스로 블루와 블랙 포인트를 더하여 일본의 이미지를 표현합니다.

2 color combination

3 color combination

4 color combination

Japanese Green tea

Green tea is tea made by picking tea leaves and steaming them immediately or by boiling them in a pot. Since green tea does not go through the fermentation process, the ingredients of the tea remain intact, so vitamin C is five to eight times the amount of lemon. It contains a large amount of catechin, which indicates the prevention and suppression effects of various diseases, such as anti-aging, cancer prevention, and food poisoning.

Japanese springs

There are thousands of hot springs in Japan, which are related to the large number of volcanoes in Japan. Hot springs are the surface of the earth due to the heat of the ground, as the temperature around the volcano is very high.

Sushi generally refers to putting fresh fish on rice made by mixing salt, vinegar and sugar, and dipping it in wasabi soy sauce. It is not clear when sushi was started, but there are theories that it was introduced to store fish when it began to eat fish, and that it was introduced when rice farming began. There are many theories about the origin of sushi, but it is estimated that Japanese sushi was created due to the influence of Southeast Asia, where fish storage methods and dishes using them have been developed.

Japanese sushi

Learn about Traditional Japanese Culture

Kimono is a traditional Japanese costume. Today, kimono is often worn by women when there are special events such as ceremonies and weddings.

SEASONAL

SEASONAL

Spring

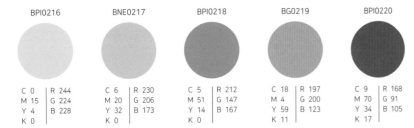

BPI0216	BNE0217	BPI0218	BG0219	BPI0220
C 0 / R 244	C 6 / R 230	C 5 / R 212	C 18 / R 197	C 9 / R 168
M 15 / G 224	M 20 / G 206	M 51 / G 147	M 4 / G 200	M 70 / G 91
Y 4 / B 228	Y 32 / B 173	Y 14 / B 167	Y 59 / B 123	Y 34 / B 105
K 0	K 0	K 0	K 11	K 17

Color Palette - Light Pink, Cream Beige, Pink, Light Olive Green, Dark Pink
따뜻한 햇살에 생명력이 피어나는 봄은 밝고 화사하며 부드럽고 온화합니다.
핑크, 베이지, 그린 배색은 귀엽고 발랄하며 생기 있는 봄을 표현합니다.

2 color combination   3 color combination   4 color combination

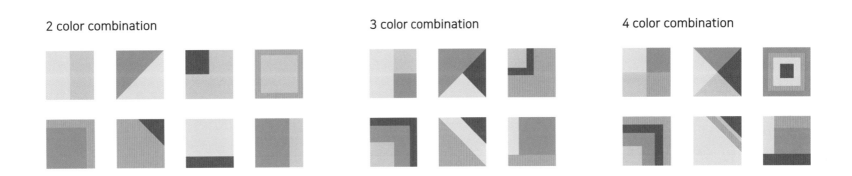

Cherry blossoms in spring

Cherry blossoms are flowers that bloom in Oriental cherry. Having pink or white petals that bloom brightly in spring.

The flower language means 'the fleetingness and beauty of life, purity, outstanding beauty, beauty of the world, mental beauty, refinement, wealth, and prosperity.'

SPRING, THE SEASON OF STRAWBERRIES

Strawberries grow briskly in spring after the winter, and flowers bloom and bear fruit. The ripe strawberries are vivid red with a freshing and sweet taste. Spring strawberries have the effect of beautifying the skin and purifying the blood.

The pigment called anthocyanin, the red color of strawberries, has anti-cancer effects and is high in pectin, a dietary fiber, which lowers cholesterol levels. Strawberries contain a lot of lycopene, which is usually contained in red fruits, which can help prevent aging by enhancing immunity and strengthening blood vessels.

SPRING GREEN LEAVES

Sprout vegetables do not refer to specific vegetables, but to harvest young leaves or stems obtained by sowing seeds of vegetables or grains and to be eaten fresh. It is usually a young vegetable with one to three main leaves that sprout from a seed.

THE BRIDE OF SPRING

Spring is a good season to get married. The warm and fresh season is not only good for weddings, but also makes the beautiful bride shine brighter.

Summer

BB0221	BB0222	BB0223	BG0224	BY0225
C 18 R 220	C 60 R 133	C 96 R 34	C 34 R 190	C 0 R 247
M 0 G 237	M 0 G 195	M 35 G 111	M 0 G 217	M 12 G 218
Y 0 B 250	Y 13 B 215	Y 0 B 168	Y 34 B 184	Y 70 B 104
K 0	K 0	K 14	K 0	K 0

Color Palette - Light Blue, Pool Blue, Strong Blue, Mint Green, Light Mellow Yellow

싱그러움과 푸르름이 가득한 여름은 투명하고 찬란하며 맑고 산뜻합니다.
블루와 그린을 베이스로 옐로 색상을 포인트로 배색하여 시원하고 경쾌한 여름을 표현합니다.

2 color combination

3 color combination

4 color combination

Hot but clear summer weather

Summer is the second of the four seasons, after spring, and refers to the hottest season before fall. Entering June, the sun's altitude increases and the sun becomes stronger, and the day gets longer and longer to summer solstice, so the temperature continues to rise.

01

Boracay Island is famous for its summer travel destination. Travelers from Germany and Switzerland found it in the 1970s. In the early days, it was mainly visited by Europeans, who later became a world-class resort, widely known for its fine sand and clean beaches. There are about a dozen beaches, including White Beach and Pukashell Beach. It is equipped with various marine sports and leisure facilities such as horseback riding and golf, and you can dive all year round. There are motorcycles and tricycles as transportation means.

How to enjoy various flavors of ice cream

Water-play preparations

02

What you need most to enjoy playing in the water is swimsuits. It is also good to prepare a life jacket to enjoy water play safely in deep water. Be sure to prepare sunscreen, hats, and sunglasses as your skin may burn during water play.

Autumn

BNE0226	BNE0227	BBR0228	BBR0229	BBR0230

C 6 · R 236 M 11 · G 224 Y 23 · B 198 K 0	C 14 · R 213 M 24 · G 191 Y 44 · B 149 K 0	C 8 · R 188 M 40 · G 144 Y 75 · B 76 K 14	C 17 · R 132 M 46 · G 103 Y 56 · B 80 K 39	C 17 · R 120 M 82 · G 58 Y 81 · B 43 K 40

Color Palette   Light Beige, Sand Beige, Yellow Brown, Brown, Red Brown
풍요로운 황금빛이 떠오르는 가을은 따뜻하고 안정적이며 포근합니다.
베이지와 브라운의 유사 색상 배색으로 편안하고 온화한 가을을 표현합니다.

2 color combination

3 color combination

4 color combination

Autumnal sentiment

Autumn is a season of satisfaction because of the joy of harvest, In addition, the weather is cool in autumn, which emphasizes the need for reading, Autumn is called "the season of falling leaves," and one can see a picture of life from the leaves that fall, Autumn leaves and autumn morning fogs are all words that represent futility, expressing the sentiments of the season, The reason why there are so many expressions referring to the elderly in autumn is because they thought that the old age of life corresponds to the fall,

Autumn memories

Deep night, the moon reminds me of memories, The wind is blowing and standing alone in the moonlight, I look back on my past memories, Life is a beautiful thing, I remember those days, I know what happiness is, The memory comes back to life as the wind flows,

Candles and mood lights are also used as props for the autumn mood, When you light a scented candle, the flickering of the flame and the subtle scent go well with the calm and tranquil autumn atmosphere, The mood light is bright and soft enough not to be dark, so it is good for interior use, It is good for sleeping or auxiliary lighting at night in a bedroom, Candlelight is a candle-shaped mood light that can create a subtle atmosphere, Candles are easily extinguished and dangerous as they can fall into your hands, but candlelights are light and easy to carry, Good for interior use or event use,

Autumn atmosphere

Stay in the sunshine on a clear Autumn days

In autumn, when we suddenly miss someone or walk on the road alone, even if it's someone passing by, we want to meet a beautiful person like maple leaves,

117

Winter

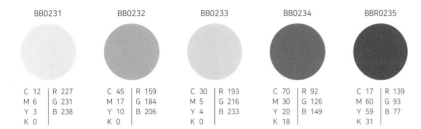

BB0231	BB0232	BB0233	BB0234	BBR0235
C 12 R 227	C 45 R 159	C 30 R 193	C 70 R 92	C 17 R 139
M 6 G 231	M 17 G 184	M 5 G 216	M 30 G 126	M 60 G 93
Y 3 B 238	Y 10 B 206	Y 4 B 233	Y 20 B 149	Y 59 B 77
K 0	K 0	K 0	K 18	K 31

Color Palette - Light Pale Blue, Light Steel Blue, Sky Blue, Light Indigo Blue, Cinamon Brown
순백의 흰 눈이 내리는 겨울은 차갑고 고요하며 깊은 어둠 속 고독이 있는 계절입니다.
블루 톤 온 톤 배색에 브라운을 포인트로 주어 차분하고 심플한 겨울 이미지를 표현합니다.

2 color combination   3 color combination   4 color combination

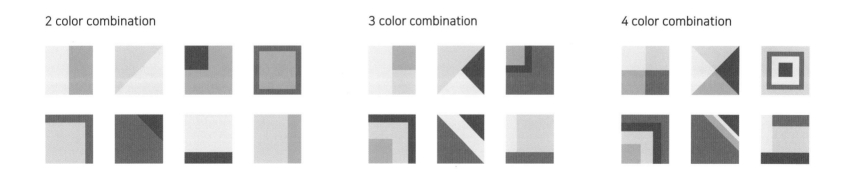

Traveling to the Winterland

Things you need to stay warm in winter

Gloves mean a pocket-shaped hand-wrap for the purpose of protecting the hand, keeping the hand warm, showing hand signals, and class symbol. Formally, it is distinguished as a mitten that separates only the glove and thumb. Mitten also refers to long gloves for women with no fingertips.

Mufflers means to be worn around the neck for the purpose of keeping warm, dustproof, or decoration. Depending on the method of use, it can also be used as a shoulder cover. Materials include silk, wool, chemical fiber, fur, and textiles, and there are various types depending on size, shape, and use.

Do you want to build a Snowman with someone?

How to build a lovely snowman

A snowman begins by making two or more large snowballs. Generally, it makes the snowball at the bottom bigger. If additional decorations are used as accessories, use branches or leaves that are readily available around them. It is easy to make arms with branches, and make eyes with leaves. They also put a scarf, gloves, and a hat on them.

Sweet Dessert

Marshmallow is a sponge-type candy food. It was commercialized in the 19th century in Europe in the current form of snacks, and has a sponge-like tissue that is flexible and elastic enough to maintain its shape. The marshmallow is baked by stirring together sugar, syrup, flavoring, gelatin, and starch, then rolled in fine sugar powder or corn flour. You can eat something that is cut into bite-sized pieces, put it on a dish as an ornament, or put it on a stick and grill it. Marshmallow is put in cakes and cookies as well as Rocky Road and ice cream.

Tropical

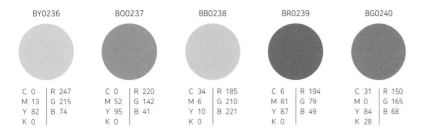

BY0236		BO0237		BB0238		BR0239		BG0240	
C 0	R 247	C 0	R 220	C 34	R 185	C 6	R 194	C 31	R 150
M 13	G 215	M 52	G 142	M 6	G 210	M 81	G 79	M 0	G 165
Y 82	B 74	Y 95	B 41	Y 10	B 221	Y 87	B 49	Y 84	B 68
K 0		K 0		K 0		K 0		K 28	

Color Palette - Canary Yellow, Carrot Orange, Sky Blue, Orange Red, Olive Green
Tropical은 '열대의, 열대성의'라는 뜻으로 뜨거운 태양과 바다, 색색의 열대과일이 연상됩니다.
채도가 높은 컬러의 톤 인 톤 배색으로 열대의 컬러풀하고 팝한 이미지를 표현합니다.

2 color combination

3 color combination

4 color combination

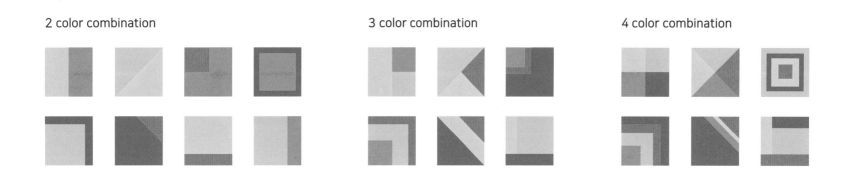

Tropical fruits

How to eat

Tropical fruits can make juice, ice cream, sherbet, etc. Tropical fruits are also used in the food industry. Dried tropical fruits are used to make flour, bread, cheese, and snacks.

There are many ways to eat tropical fruits. You can make and eat various desserts such as jam, jelly, juice, ice cream, sherbet, etc. using tropical fruits. Tropical fruits are also applied to the food industry. Dried tropical fruits are made into flour and made into dough, or used as ingredients such as bread, cheese, and cookies.

Tropical drinks

The common way to eat fruit is to eat raw. But in hot summers and resorts, tropical fruits are more often eaten as juice to quench thirst and satisfy nutrients. The way to make juice is to crush or grind fruits, fill them with ice, preserve the taste of fresh fruits, or add a small amount of sugar to make it.

The palm tree is a tropical tree belonging to the palm family, which has several species and provides various food ingredients such as coconut, palm sprouts, and palm hearts. The starch extracted from the stalks of palm trees makes sago, and some kinds of palm trees also provide sugar, oil and vegetable butter.

Harvest

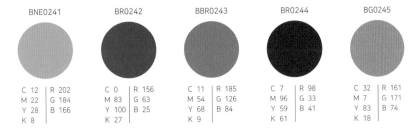

BNE0241	BR0242	BBR0243	BR0244	BG0245
C 12 R 202	C 0 R 156	C 11 R 185	C 7 R 98	C 32 R 161
M 22 G 184	M 83 G 63	M 54 G 126	M 96 G 33	M 7 G 171
Y 28 B 166	Y 100 B 25	Y 68 B 84	Y 59 B 41	Y 83 B 74
K 8	K 27	K 9	K 61	K 18

Color Palette - Light Cocoa, Dark Orange Red, Orange Brown, Dark Red, Olive Green
Harvest는 잘 익은 곡식과 열매, 풍요로운 가을의 이미지를 떠오르게 합니다.
채도가 낮은 붉은 톤 색상을 베이스로 그린으로 포인트를 주어 수확의 이미지를 표현합니다.

2 color combination

3 color combination

4 color combination

01

Potatoes

Potatoes are generally generic for crops that store large amounts of carbohydrates in the root or root stem of a plant. Potatoes that are important as alternative food include potatoes, sweet potatoes, taro, cassava, and yamma. Potatoes are relatively less easily grown and easier to harvest, so it is assumed that they have long been grown and used as staple food regardless of season in the tropics.

02

full of plenty of seasonal fruits and vegetables

03

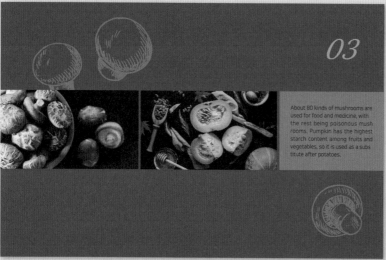

About 80 kinds of mushrooms are used for food and medicine, with the rest being poisonous mushrooms. Pumpkin has the highest starch content among fruits and vegetables, so it is used as a substitute after potatoes.

Grains has long been widely used as the most important food of all foods.

What is obtained from plants as food materials for humans is called grains, such as rice, barley, beans, millet, sorghum, wheat, corn, etc. Rice, wheat, and corn are the most commonly used food in the world. The grain consists mainly of starch and is light in taste, making it suitable for the staple food. In addition, the cultivation period is limited, but it can be widely cultivated, has a large quantity, has low moisture content, and is covered with a hard shell, making it easy to handle and store long-term products.

Halloween

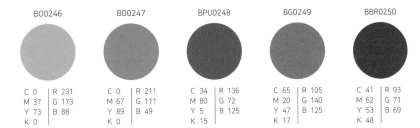

B00246	B00247	BPU0248	BG0249	BBR0250
C 0 R 231	C 0 R 211	C 34 R 136	C 65 R 105	C 41 R 93
M 37 G 173	M 67 G 111	M 80 G 72	M 20 G 140	M 62 G 71
Y 73 B 88	Y 89 B 49	Y 5 B 125	Y 47 B 125	Y 53 B 69
K 0	K 0	K 15	K 17	K 48

Color Palette - Cream Orange, Orange, Purple, Teal Green, Dark Brown

10월 31일 핼러윈(Halloween) 축제에는 잭오랜턴, 유령쿠키, 거미와 박쥐 모형들로 장식을 합니다.
잭오랜턴을 상징하는 오렌지와 대비되는 퍼플, 그린 배색으로 핼러윈 축제 분위기를 표현합니다.

2 color combination

3 color combination

4 color combination

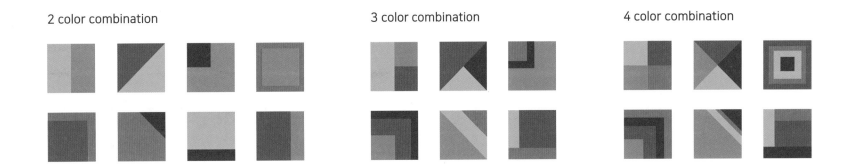

Halloween Day

Halloween is a festival held every October 31st and the day before All Saints' Day across the United States. Originally, Halloween was known to originate from the Celtic traditional festival 'Samhain'. On the last day of the year, the Celts comforted the souls of the dead and chased away evil spirits by preparing food and offering an offer to the Deathly Hallows.

Trick or treat

As a representative event of Halloween, children dress up as witches, fairies, ghosts, and characters in popular cartoons and go from house to house to get candy or snacks is called 'trick or treat'. It is presumed that this originated from medieval customs. In the Middle Ages, on Catholic festivals in Great Britain and Ireland, children or poor people came to sing and recite prayers for the dead, and people gave them a small cake called 'soul cake' in return.

Making Jack-O-Lanterns and then light candles inside

Jack O'Lantern is a pumpkin lamp that appears on Halloween Day. A large pumpkin hollowed out with the face of a goblin, and a candle inside it to make it look like a goblin's eye.

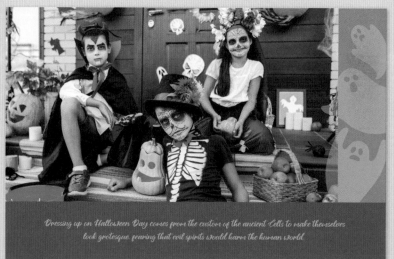

Dressing up on Halloween Day comes from the custom of the ancient Celts to make themselves look grotesque, fearing that evil spirits would harm the human world.

125

Christmas

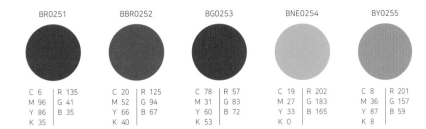

BR0251	BBR0252	BG0253	BNE0254	BY0255
C 6 / R 135	C 20 / R 125	C 78 / R 57	C 19 / R 202	C 8 / R 201
M 96 / G 41	M 52 / G 94	M 31 / G 83	M 27 / G 183	M 36 / G 157
Y 86 / B 35	Y 66 / B 67	Y 60 / B 72	Y 33 / B 165	Y 87 / B 59
K 35	K 40	K 53	K 0	K 8

Color Palette - Deep Red, Brown, Deep Green, Light Cocoa, Golden Yellow
크리스마스를 상징하는 색상은 산타클로스의 레드와 크리스마스 트리의 그린입니다.
저채도의 레드, 그린, 브라운 배색은 따뜻하고 포근한 크리스마스 분위기를 연출합니다.

2 color combination

3 color combination

4 color combination

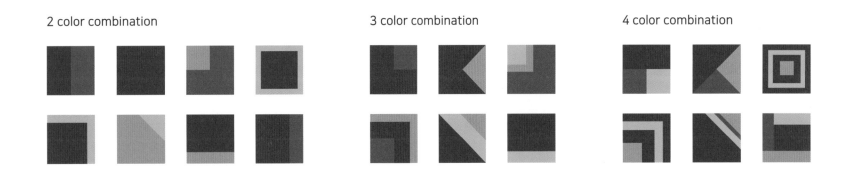

Wishing You a very Merry Christmas

In December, there is a special day that many people look forward to regardless of religion, It's Christmas, December 25th, On Christmas, we say thank you to God for sending us Jesus and exchange gifts to share the joy, On Christmas day, people exchange gifts and letters with close people and express their gratitude throughout the year.

Hope you have wonderful Holidays

May the good times and treasures of the present become the golden memories of tomorrow, Wishing you lots of love, joy and happiness, The gift of love, The gift of peace, The gift of happiness, May all these be yours at Christmas,

Happy Merry Christmas

Love and best wishes for merry Christmas and a wonderful new year!

May the Christmas season fill your home with joy, your heart with love, and your life with laughter.

Valentine

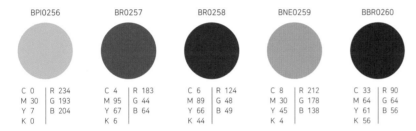

BPI0256	BR0257	BR0258	BNE0259	BBR0260
C 0 R 234	C 4 R 183	C 6 R 124	C 8 R 212	C 33 R 90
M 30 G 193	M 95 G 44	M 89 G 48	M 30 G 178	M 64 G 64
Y 7 B 204	Y 67 B 64	Y 66 B 49	Y 45 B 138	Y 61 B 56
K 0	K 6	K 44	K 4	K 56

Color Palette - Soft Pink, Pink Red, Dark Red, Warm Beige, Deep Brown
밸런타인데이는 사랑하는 사람에게 초콜릿을 선물하는 기념일입니다.
설렘을 담은 핑크, 레드 컬러에 초콜릿을 상징하는 짙은 브라운 배색으로 로맨틱 무드를 표현합니다.

2 color combination   3 color combination   4 color combination

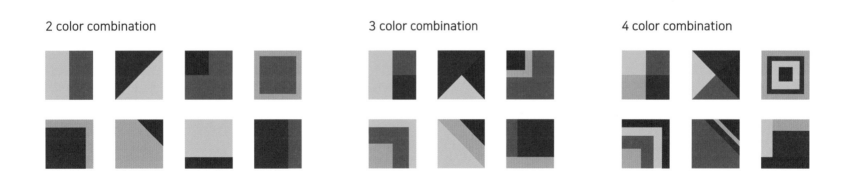

Happy Valentine's Day

You are the finest, loveliest, tenderest, and most beautiful person I have ever known and even that is an understatement.

I am very indecisive and I always have a hard time picking
my favorite anythings. But I know for sure that you are my favorite.

The day to present flowers and candies to someone you love.

In the third century, Roman marriages were possible under the permission of the emperor, and Valentine was the name of a priest who was martyred for making each other's beloved young people marry without the emperor's permission. After his martyrdom, he designated this day as a holiday and celebrated it every year as a lover's day.

Valentine's Day, February 14, is considered a day when women confess their love to their favorite man. The main medium for delivering love is chocolate. Recently, more and more people are preparing their own unique gifts. Using Valentine's Day, it became a very beautiful thing just for men and women to honestly confess their feelings to each other.

Chocolate

On February 14, 1477, a young English woman sent a love letter to a man she had a crush on, which led to the marriage of the two. Since the news was made public, February 14 has become the day when lovers confess their love. Motogomi bakery, a Japanese confectionery company, sold various chocolates on Valentine's Day under the phrase "Tell Love with Chocolate," which is the beginning of Valentine's Day.

Sweet, Love Romance

The real lover is the one who can thrill you by kissing your forehead or smiling into your eyes or just staring into space.

Fireworks

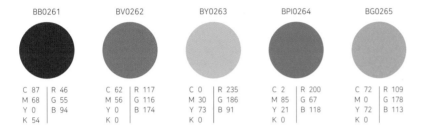

BB0261		BV0262		BY0263		BPI0264		BG0265	
C 87	R 46	C 62	R 117	C 0	R 235	C 2	R 200	C 72	R 109
M 68	G 55	M 56	G 116	M 30	G 186	M 85	G 67	M 0	G 178
Y 0	B 94	Y 0	B 174	Y 73	B 91	Y 21	B 118	Y 72	B 113
K 54		K 0		K 0		K 0		K 0	

Color Palette - Navy Blue, Iris Violet, Light Orange Yellow, Hot Pink, Clover Green
축제를 상징하는 불꽃놀이는 색색의 컬러로 어두운 밤하늘을 화려하게 장식합니다.
채도가 높은 컬러풀한 색상을 톤 인 톤 배색하여 선명하고 개성 강한 이미지를 연출합니다.

2 color combination

3 color combination

4 color combination

The fireworks, which can be seen in the night festival for entertainment today, were invented about 1,000 years ago in China, which resulted from the invention of gunpowder in the ninth century. At religious festivals, a bamboo tube filled with gunpowder was thrown into the fire and exploded, apparently based on the superstition that the sound of the explosion would drive away evil spirits. There is a high possibility that some of these small bombs produced gas and flew up like a rocket.

Splendid fireworks festival

Fireworks have the power to move people's minds, so people can shoot firecrackers at the peak of the event to catch other people's eyes. The flame that blooms brilliantly against the dark night sky is magical. However, this beautiful sight is actually an achievement of technology. To make beautiful fireworks and shoot fireworks, gunpowder is needed.

Colorful Stars

Fireworks do not just give pleasure. Burning firecrackers can cause ozone. Also, the metal powder used for fireworks may fall and get into the human eye, so it is recommended to enjoy the fireworks a little further away.

Fireworks were made in only one yellow color for 700 years after its invention, and around 1800 a new color of fireworks was developed when French chemist Claude Bertolle discovered potassium chlorate.

RED, YELLOW, PURPLE, ORANGE, BLUE GREEN
DARK RED, YELLOW GREEN AND SO ON.

Colorful fireworks are called stars. Small stars burn fast and make small sparks, while big stars burn slowly and fall like waterfalls.

How to enjoy the fireworks display

In order to get a good view of the fireworks, it is recommended to move to high-lying hills or buildings, or to a wide open river or lawn. It is also good to make a wish while enjoying fireworks with your family, friends, lovers, and others.

Aurora

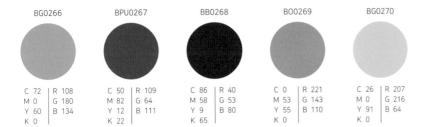

BG0266	BPU0267	BB0268	BO0269	BG0270
C 72 R 108	C 50 R 109	C 86 R 40	C 0 R 221	C 26 R 207
M 0 G 180	M 82 G 64	M 58 G 53	M 53 G 143	M 0 G 216
Y 60 B 134	Y 12 B 111	Y 9 B 80	Y 55 B 110	Y 91 B 64
K 0	K 22	K 65	K 0	K 0

Color Palette - Clover Green, Purple, Midnight Blue, Peach Orange, Yellow Green

오로라(Aurora)는 '새벽'이란 뜻의 라틴어로, 깊은 밤하늘에 방대한 빛을 그려냅니다.
어둠 속에서도 빛나는 차가운 빛의 파장을 그린, 퍼플, 오렌지로 배색하여 신비한 분위기를 연출합니다.

2 color combination

3 color combination

4 color combination

Aurora,
a gift from heaven

Yellowknife

Yellowknife is located in the southern part of the Macken zie district of Canada, on the north side of Lake Great Sla ve, and on the coast of the Yellowknife River estuary. It is known as a place where you can see beautiful aurora.

Just because you came to Yellowknife doesn't mean you can see the aurora right away. During the day, people enjoy activities such as relaxation, sightseeing in the city, and riding dog sleds at Yellowknife, and at night, they take a car to Aurora Village to observe the aurora.

The wavelengths of light

Aurora is a phenomenon in which charged particles entering Earth from space collide with gases from high-rise atmosphere and glow. Electron particles that fall into the atmosphere along the Earth's magnetic force line collide with atoms or molecules in the atmosphere, causing excited gases to emit light as they return to their original bottom state.

When you visually observe aurora, you see a lot of green aurora. This is because it produces the most light equivalent to 557.7 nm, the most sensitive wavelength for our eyes. Various colors of aurora are possible because the falling particles of aeration into the atmosphere collide with different gases in the atmosphere.

133

BUSINESS

SECTION 7

BUSINESS

Global

Environment

Expert

Innovation

Start-up

Service

Global

BGY0271	BB0272	BB0273	BB0274	BB0275
C 18 R 211	C 63 R 124	C 85 R 67	C 54 R 133	C 34 R 188
M 13 G 212	M 4 G 187	M 46 G 108	M 22 G 159	M 0 G 221
Y 12 B 213	Y 9 B 216	Y 6 B 159	Y 22 B 171	Y 0 B 246
K 0	K 0	K 10	K 7	K 0

Color Palette - Light Gray, Pool Blue, Denim Blue, Stone Blue, Sky Blue

다양한 분야에서 교류가 많아지는 비즈니스의 세계화는 광대하고 빠르며, 전문화되어가고 있습니다.
디지털 문화 및 혁신과 전문성을 상징하는 블루, 그레이 배색으로 성장하는 세계화를 표현합니다.

2 color combination

3 color combination

4 color combination

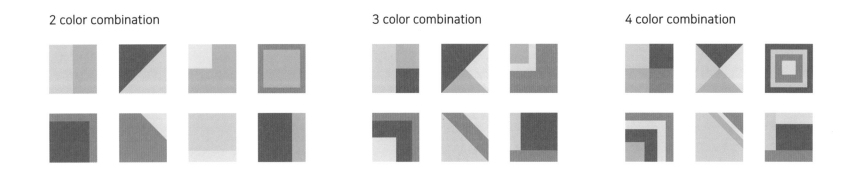

What can be gained through globalization?

GLOBALIZATION THAT CHANGES OUR LIVES

With globalization, there are many things that people all over the world can share. First of all, the trade between countries became free, so it was easy to buy and use goods made in other countries. Of course, we can easily meet the products made in our country in foreign countries.

As many countries around the world have been influencing and exchanging with each other in various fields, not only goods, but also trends and cultures have spread easily. It is also a globalization that people all over the world enjoy listening to the same music and watching the same movie.

ECONOMIC EXCHANGES AND PROBLEMS OF GLOBALIZATION

HOW CAN WE SOLVE THESE PROBLEMS

Each country should be able to interact on an equal footing. It is also important to ensure that everyone can enjoy the benefits of globalization. Furthermore, in order for globalization to become a conduit for developing various cultures, it is necessary to introduce the cultures of various countries without discrimination and to recognize the characteristics of each culture with an open mind.

TRADE EXPANSION

The first step in globalization began with the exchange of resources and goods from each country. Each country has a lot of resources and products produced according to the environment, and the remaining ones have been sold to other countries and started to buy what was lacking, resulting in trade. The development of transportation and communication made this exchange faster.

Environment

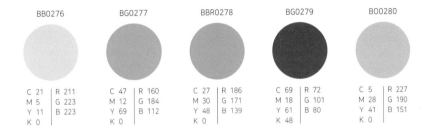

BB0276	BG0277	BBR0278	BG0279	BO0280
C 21 / R 211	C 47 / R 160	C 27 / R 186	C 69 / R 72	C 5 / R 227
M 5 / G 223	M 12 / G 184	M 30 / G 171	M 18 / G 101	M 28 / G 190
Y 11 / B 223	Y 69 / B 112	Y 48 / B 139	Y 61 / B 80	Y 41 / B 151
K 0	K 0	K 0	K 48	K 0

Color Palette - Light Green Blue, Froggy Green, Light Khaki Brown, Deep Green, Light Orange
산업화로 인해 발생한 환경 문제에 대한 연구와 해결 방안이 주요 이슈 및 비즈니스로 자리 잡고 있습니다.
자연을 상징하는 그린, 블루, 브라운에 새로운 발상을 표현하는 오렌지를 배색하여 환경연구를 표현합니다.

2 color combination

3 color combination

4 color combination

Protection of the environment

Environmental pollution on a global scale is not just a natural phenomenon, but a combination of natural factors for artificial causes. Environmental destruction is different from natural disasters that cannot control the occurrence itself, and controlling social factors can prevent the occurrence itself in principle. Preventing the cause of the outbreak is the basis of preventing environmental destruction.

Eco-friendly Products

Environment-friendly means not polluting or destroying the natural environment, but harmonizing well with the natural environment. Eco-friendly activities that can be practiced in everyday life include using shopping bags or eco bags instead of plastic bags, and carrying tumblers instead of disposable cups.

Recycling refers to the reuse of used items as raw materials or materials into products for their original or close use. Reuse means the various or additional use of an item while maintaining its original intention at the time of purchase. For example, using an empty coke bottle as a water bottle or using newspapers for packaging is a reuse option. Recycling not only can overcome the scarcity of resources through reproduction of waste materials but also contribute to environmental conservation as it can reasonably and economically treat wastes that are factors of pollution.

Recycling
for the Environment

What should we do to save the green planet

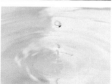

If simulations can predict environmental degradation in advance and review pollutants or regulatory methods, the worst could be prevented.

Expert

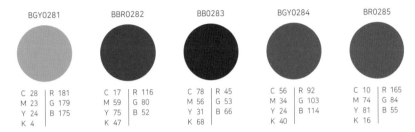

BGY0281	BBR0282	BB0283	BGY0284	BR0285
C 28 R 181	C 17 R 116	C 78 R 45	C 56 R 92	C 10 R 165
M 23 G 179	M 59 G 80	M 56 G 53	M 34 G 103	M 74 G 84
Y 24 B 175	Y 75 B 52	Y 31 B 66	Y 24 B 114	Y 81 B 55
K 4	K 47	K 68	K 40	K 16

Color Palette - Gray, Brown, Midnight Blue, Dark Blue Gray, Dark Orange Red

전문가는 비즈니스 및 기타 특정 업무와 영역에서 전문적인 지식과 능력이 있는 사람을 의미합니다.
저채도의 그레이, 브라운, 블루에 레드를 포인트로 넣어 지적이고 열정적인 전문 지식인의 이미지를 표현합니다.

2 color combination

3 color combination

4 color combination

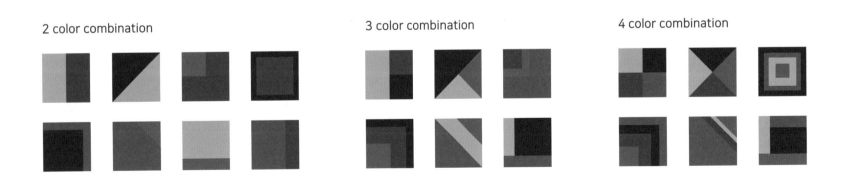

Big Data Analysts

As Gartner Group, a market research firm, selected Big Data as one of the world's top 10 technologies in 2012, attention was drawn to its job as a big data analyst. Big data analysts are responsible for reading trends in numerous data and producing high-value-added results. It also manages and analyzes large amounts of big data to predict people's behavior patterns and market economic conditions. You can also identify the other person's tendency by text messages or keywords that you send and receive on social media such as Facebook and Twitter.

INSURANCE COUNSELORS

Life planners

An insurance planner shall refer to a person registered in accordance with the provisions of the Insurance Business Act as a broker of the conclusion of an insurance contract for an insurance company, including non-corporate divisions and foundations.

The work of insurance planners is expanding beyond simple recruitment to the financial design of households such as financial counseling, life design, and loan counseling on loans. They need to have extensive financial knowledge as they need to conduct financial consultations linked to insurance products, fund design for retirement protection, and consultation on household loans or housing loans.

Merchandisers, Specialize in product planning

Merchandisers is also known as 'MD' for short. Merchandisers are professionals in charge of product planning and sales. They have the right to decide on merchandising plans, purchases, processing, product display, sales, and so on, and are also responsible for it.

STRATEGIC MANAGEMENT TO ACHIEVE GOALS.

Strategic experts are responsible for the entire process of analyzing external environments and internal situations to establish, implement and evaluate strategies accordingly in order to maximize the performance of the enterprise.

Innovation

BGY0286	BGY0287	BB0288	BB0289	BB0290

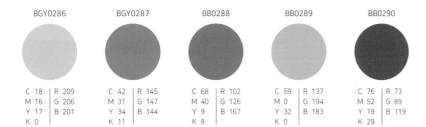

C 18	R 209	C 42	R 145	C 68	R 102	C 59	R 137	C 76	R 73
M 16	G 206	M 31	G 147	M 40	G 126	M 0	G 194	M 52	G 89
Y 17	B 201	Y 34	B 144	Y 9	B 167	Y 32	B 183	Y 19	B 119
K 0		K 11		K 8		K 0		K 29	

Color Palette - Light Beige Gray, Steel Gray, Sea Blue, Light Turquoise Blue, Dark Blue
Innovation(혁신)은 새로운 기술 또는 방법을 도입하여 얻은 획기적인 변화와 경제적 발전을 뜻합니다.
그레이와 블루 계열 색상 배색으로 새로운 도약과 이상을 실현할 창조적인 이미지를 표현합니다.

2 color combination

3 color combination

4 color combination

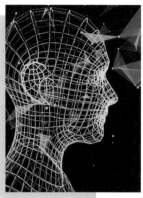

01

Artificial Intelligence

Artificial intelligence is a technology that realizes human learning ability, reasoning ability, perceptual ability, and understanding of natural language through computer programs. Artificial intelligence is a field of computer science and information technology that studies how computers can think, learn, and develop human intelligence. Also, artificial intelligence does not exist in itself, but has many direct and indirect implications for other areas of computer science.

02

Autonomous driving is a futuristic car technology that moves on its own without the driver driving.

03

Innovation is to discover new products, services, and new ways and apply them to management activities. Innovation is made by the interactive and interconstrained relationship between technology and management.

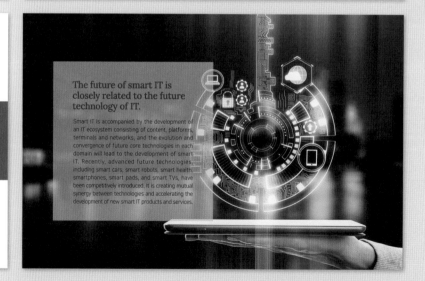

The future of smart IT is closely related to the future technology of IT.

Smart IT is accompanied by the development of an IT ecosystem consisting of content, platforms, terminals and networks, and the evolution and convergence of future core technologies in each domain will lead to the development of smart IT. Recently, advanced future technologies, including smart cars, smart robots, smart health, smartphones, smart pads, and smart TVs, have been competitively introduced. It is creating mutual synergy between technologies and accelerating the development of new smart IT products and services.

Start-up

	BBR0291		BY0292		BB0293		BR0294		BB0295

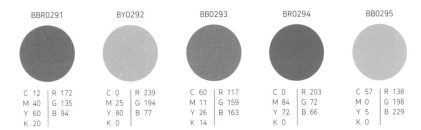

C 12	R 172	C 0	R 239	C 60	R 117	C 0	R 203	C 57	R 138
M 40	G 135	M 25	G 194	M 11	G 159	M 84	G 72	M 0	G 198
Y 60	B 94	Y 80	B 77	Y 26	B 163	Y 72	B 66	Y 5	B 229
K 20		K 0		K 14		K 0		K 0	

Color Palette - Camel Brown, Light Orange Yellow, Peacock Blue, Orange Red, Pool Blue
Start-up은 혁신적인 기술과 아이디어를 보유한 신생 창업 기업을 지칭합니다.
컬러풀한 옐로, 블루, 레드, 브라운 배색으로 다채로운 아이디어와 새로운 시작을 표현합니다.

2 color combination

3 color combination

4 color combination

Start-up

Startup means a start-up company. It was first used in Silicon Valley in the United States. Although it usually has innovative technologies and ideas, it often lacks funding, and it is a technology and Internet-based company with high risk, high profit, and high growth potential. A startup with a corporate value of more than $1 billion is called a unicorn.

Start-up Accelerato

It is an organization that finds new start-ups at a stage where only start-up ideas and items exist and plays a role in supporting non-core tasks such as work space, marketing, and public relations. Startup accelerators not only provide offices and consulting services to start-ups, but also connect global experts in various fields such as marketing and strategy as mentors. This is similar to venture incubators, but there is a difference in that it is institutions or companies that support early start-up companies right after their start-ups, ahead of accelerators.

Organizations
creating new products
and services

Start-up companies generally work in a free working environment, which forms the basis of a startup culture. According to a 1960 paper published by Douglas McGregor, reward and punishment in the working environment is not necessary to increase work efficiency, and this factor may be a hindrance to work efficiency. A free working environment helps workers concentrate more on their work.

A Start-up refers to a company that has just started its business. It refers to a technology-oriented company with great growth potential that can be evaluated as future value rather than current value. In addition, they should have a real company, not a team.

Service

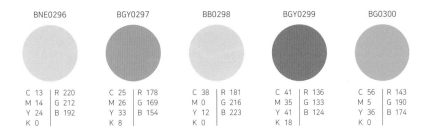

BNE0296	BGY0297	BB0298	BGY0299	BG0300
C 13 R 220	C 25 R 178	C 38 R 181	C 41 R 136	C 56 R 143
M 14 G 212	M 26 G 169	M 0 G 216	M 35 G 133	M 5 G 190
Y 24 B 192	Y 33 B 154	Y 12 B 223	Y 41 B 124	Y 36 B 174
K 0	K 8	K 0	K 18	K 0

Color Palette - Beige, Warm Gray, Mint Blue, Steel Gray, Aqua Green

서비스는 생산된 재화를 운반하거나 생산, 소비에 필요한 인력을 제공하는 것을 뜻합니다.
웜 톤의 베이지, 그레이에 블루, 그린으로 포인트를 주어 편안하고 안정적인 이미지를 심어줍니다.

What Can I Help You With?

2 color combination

3 color combination

4 color combination

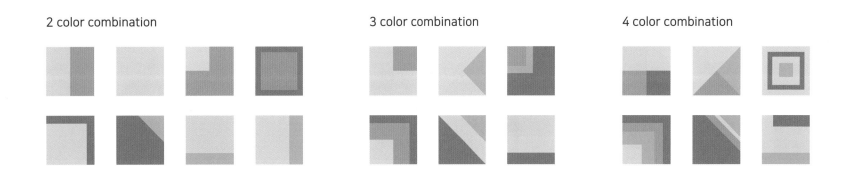

Telemarketing Call Center Counsellors

Telephone counselors create value not only by simply answering calls, but also by responding to customers related to marketing and service, etc. If necessary, it also serves as a fundraiser for the organization or as a help desk inside and outside the organization.

01

Medical services refer to services that are subject to the treatment, nursing, prevention, management and rehabilitation of diseases and to comprehensive services including maintenance and promotion of health. Health care workers are suppliers of services and are supported by public organizations, private organizations, local and national administrative agencies to effectively function. The service must be of high quality, require the high level of knowledge, professional skills and skills of health care workers, and must have sufficient resources for talent, materials, and economic power.

Perfect cleaning service provided by experts

Package Delivery

02

Package delivery is a direct transport to the place where individuals or businesses require packaged goods. In general, the service is limited to transportation within the country, but international logistics companies handle international courier services.

147

■ **BOOKTORY**

북토리디자인센터

종합 인쇄 브랜드 북토리는 인쇄 디자인 역량을 집중적으로 강화하기 위해 북토리디자인센터를 운영하고 있습니다. 북토리디자인센터는 인쇄물에 디자인이라는 경쟁력을 더하여 고객 만족 중심의 업무가 진행되는 것을 목표로 신설되었습니다. 우리는 고객의 제작 의도와 아이디어가 실현될 수 있도록 인쇄물의 특성과 콘셉트를 정확하게 파악하여 디자인을 제안합니다. 나아가 결과물의 완성도를 높이기 위해 업계 트렌드와 컬러 연구에 매진하고 있습니다.

북토리디자인센터에서 진행한 이번 '디자이너의 컬러 팔레트' 프로젝트는 디자이너의 고민을 해결함과 동시에 컬러의 기준을 제시하고자 시작하게 되었습니다. 색을 골라 조합하는 과정부터 인쇄용지마다 매번 달라지는 색차까지, 디자이너라면 한 번쯤은 색과 관련된 여러 어려움에 직면하게 됩니다. 오랜 집필 끝에 탄생한 이 책은 추상적인 생각과 느낌을 구체적으로 표현할 수 있도록 각 주제에 맞는 색 조합을 제안합니다. 또한 G7 Master 인증의 CMYK 관리하에 제작되어 실무 또는 감리 현장에서 컬러의 기준으로써 활용될 수 있습니다.

다양한 작업 현장에서 디자인 샘플이 필요한 실무진, 색 조합을 어려워하는 디자이너, 각종 인쇄물에서 정확하고 일관된 색을 구현해야 하는 인쇄감리 담당자에게 이 책이 유용하게 쓰이길 희망합니다.

디자이너의 컬러 팔레트 3

실무에 영감을 더하는 배색 & 톤 컬러 스타일

초판인쇄	2022년 4월 30일
초판발행	2022년 4월 30일
기 획	한도희
지 은 이	북토리디자인센터
펴 낸 이	채종준
펴 낸 곳	한국학술정보(주)
주 소	경기도 파주시 회동길 230(문발동)
전 화	031-908-3181(대표)
팩 스	031-908-3189
홈페이지	http://ebook.kstudy.com
E-mail	출판사업부 publish@kstudy.com
등 록	제일산-115호(2000. 6. 19)

ISBN   979-11-6801-188-5   14600
       979-11-6801-185-4   (세트)